TRULY TINY GARDENS

TRULY TINY GARDENS

Thomasina Tarling

Trafalgar Square Publishing

First published in the United
States of America in 1995 by
Trafalgar Square Publishing,
North Pomfret, Vermont 05053

Printed and bound in Hong Kong

First published in Great Britain in 1995 by
Conran Octopus Limited
37 Shelton Street
London WC2H 9HN

Project Editor: Caroline Davison
American Editors: Lynne O'Hara, Marjorie Dietz
Project Art Editor: Sue Storey
Text Editor: Carole McGlynn
Picture Research: Claire Taylor
Production: Mano Mylvaganam
Illustrator: Liz Pepperell
Visualizer: Jean Morley

Library of Congress Catalog Card Number:
95-60032

ISBN 1-57076-024-1

Typeset by Textype Typesetters, Cambridge

PAGE 4 *This intimate garden, with its elegant jardinière combines* Euphorbia mellifera, Heuchera 'Palace Purple' *with mixed hostas and frilly argyranthemums.*

CONTENTS

INTRODUCTION 6

COMBATING DANK AND DARK 9

TRICKS AND ILLUSIONS 17

ADORNMENTS FOR THE TINY GARDEN 27

MAKING AN ENTRANCE 37

PASSAGEWAYS AND THROUGHWAYS 47

SUNKEN GARDENS 55

TINY BACK GARDENS AND BACKYARDS 65

ELEVATED GARDENS 75

MAINTAINING TINY GARDENS 82

PLANT DIRECTORY 86

INDEX 94

ACKNOWLEDGMENTS 96

INTRODUCTION

*E*xtremely small spaces demand an unusually spacious imagination. Gardening "on the cat's forehead," to translate a Japanese expression, offers a rousing challenge, requiring more skill and determination than any other form of this art. Do not quail at the prospect of a pint-sized garden. Resolve instead to overcome the limitations of size with originality, to transform a neglected space with small perfection, or vow simply to create a stunning view, unvisited but equally enchanting.

One of the great joys of tiny gardens is the huge range of challenges you are offered, and the tremendous feeling of satisfaction when you win. Even the most mundane of front entrances has room for a tub or two, and the roof space either at the top of a building or part-way up, offers dazzling possibilities. Indeed, virtually any space from which you can see a glimpse of sky is large enough for some form of garden. If your view offers nothing but a blank wall, consider growing plants up or down it; if it seems almost lightless, remember the illuminating qualities of mirrors and white paint; if the only space on offer is outside a window, boxes can be planted with limitless, and seasonal, variety.

One of the most important rules in planning your tiny outdoor space is to be rigorously selective with your plants. When considering a mixed planting, for example, take all the seasons into the equation. Even if you seldom venture out in winter, plan a feature or a plant combination that will look good all year, and can act as a background when more colorful mixtures appear. Light-reflecting mirrors, invaluable for transforming a dark courtyard in winter, may disappear beneath exuberant foliage in summer, while stylish but austere topiary, as well as wall shrubs, may be embroidered upon by colorful climbers.

Every plant must also offer double or treble value: nothing too ephemeral can be allowed, since every inch of space is precious and must be utilized to the full. Such fleeting beauties as peonies, aubrietas or flowering cherries (*Prunus*) are not for the minuscule garden. Regard any unfamiliar plant with the discerning eye of a prospective employer or future

mother-in-law. What else does it do; is the foliage decorative; how long does it flower; is it scented; will it fit in with existing plants? Large gardens can accommodate brief, stunning displays, as splendid as an opera diva in her Wagnerian costume. In contrast, the small space calls for planting with greater staying power.

However, there is plenty of scope within these apparent limitations for variety and change. For example, ornamental urns, as well as window boxes and hanging baskets, can be used almost as flower vases, with seasonal performers popped in and replaced when their time is over. The great strength of this "movable feast" gardening lies in its versatility and seasonal freshness.

Clearly, no space nowadays is too small to be called a garden, and areas no larger than a dining-room table are often boldly described as "landscaped." Instead of complaining about lack of space or awkward situations, people achieve a garden on a minute scale whose exquisiteness would be impossible in a larger area. As most people's lives are busier than ever, small and beautifully formed is no longer a joke phrase but an attainable ideal.

LEFT *Vertical and horizontal planting brings interest to every corner of this tiny courtyard while leaving space for a small table.*

RIGHT *The elegant formality of these box corkscrews is balanced by the billowing summer flowers edging the brick pathway.*

CHAPTER ONE

COMBATING DANK AND DARK

We have all looked out onto an unloved area, such as a basement, that is dank, dispiriting or downright gloomy. Sometimes a giant tree overhangs it or a neighboring building towers alongside, turning the sky into a distant pinpoint and offering little more than a howling space for local tomcats. Before deciding how best to improve such an area, the first thing to do is to venture outside with a stout broom and plenty of garbage bags, wearing your oldest clothes, and clean the place thoroughly. Neglected spaces always become dirty, and rotting leaves, slimy stones and slug-infested corners will do nothing to inspire your gardening efforts.

When it is cleaned and washed down, inspect the area carefully and assess the level of light it receives, as this will dictate what you can do in your tiny garden. Now start to consider the possibilities. Could you suspend hanging baskets from brackets attached to the walls? Is there a wall from which to hang a trough-shaped planter? If there is not enough

ABOVE *The mood of this rather dank corner is enhanced by garden adornments, including a striking sun wall mask, and a hosta-filled pot.*

LEFT *The thick, shade-loving foliage, interspersed with colorful flowers, which shrouds this wooden gate, obscures the boundary of the garden and suggests a larger garden beyond.*

light for planting features such as these, could you install a simple wall fountain to trickle into a bowl, or do you have a piece of sculpture that could become a focal point? Could you paint a *trompe l'œil* window or pastoral scene on the most visible piece of wall? How about a mosaic along Moorish lines or a classical doorway complete with pillars? If you do not have the necessary skills yourself, why not visit the nearest art college and see if any of the students could implement your ideas for a fee? *Objets trouvés* (see page 30), the chic name for junk, can also sometimes be recycled effectively in a garden scene: chimney pots make excellent tall containers, for example, and the cast-iron hoppers from Victorian drainpipes convert to superb wall urns.

When you have decided on the form your improvements will take, set about painting as much wall as you can reach that will be visible from your windows. There are schools of thought that prefer plain, unpainted walls, particularly when the bricks are old and have character, but my feeling is that light-enhancing must take precedence here, and white walls show up green leaves most effectively. Pale, sunny yellow can also be a good choice of color, or even a sharper, more acid yellow.

WHAT TO PLANT

If the floor is wall-to-wall concrete, and you do not fancy the job of breaking it up and removing the subsequent mountain of rubble, then search for the largest trough-shaped planters you can afford in terms of both space and money. It is sometimes possible to drill holes in the concrete to provide drainage, then build raised beds made of brick or stone. Always remember to install a good layer of drainage material in the bed before

topping up with earth. This will provide a home for plants and a level change.

If, on the other hand, your dark outdoor space has bare earth, with no concrete or paving, you should add quantities of soil improvers, such as manure, peat or peat-substitute, spent hops or mushroom compost, and think about planting climbers or wall shrubs. You will need to install trellis or stretch wires across the wall in order to grow these, unless you stick to self-clinging, mostly hardy plants such as ivies, Virginia creeper (*Parthenocissus quinquefolia*), climbing hydrangea (*Hydrangea anomala petiolaris*), *Schizophragma hydrangeoides* or *Pileostegia viburnoides* (Z 7–9). (Note: the "Z" following plant names refers to the most suitable plant zone.) Other climbers and wall shrubs that are tolerant of low light levels include

chaenomeles, *Jasminum nudiflorum*, pyracantha, *Lonicera x brownii* 'Dropmore Scarlet,' *L. x tellmanniana* and *L. tragophylla*, *Parthenocissus henryana*, *Vitis coignetiae*, *Kerria japonica* 'Pleniflora,' and *Akebia quinata*.

The bones of a dank and dark space should always be foliage plants, mainly evergreen for year-round pleasure, which are spiced with flowers as an extra. Degrees of darkness vary, but the following, mostly hardy shrubs are all tolerant of fairly deep to moderate shade: *Fatsia japonica* (Z 8–10), aucuba, box (*Buxus sempervirens*), camellias, *Daphne laureola*, elaeagnus, *Euonymus fortunei*, gaultherias, hollies, mahonias, *Lonicera nitida*, *Prunus laurocerasus* and *P. lusitanica*, pieris, kalmia and rhododendrons, sarcococcas, skimmias, *Viburnum acerifolium* and *V. davidii* (Z 7–9) as well as vincas, sasas, yews and many bamboos (species of *Arundinaria* and *Phyllostachys*). Other, mainly herbaceous, plants that are shade-tolerant and also offer flowering interest, include anemones, bergenias, cimicifugas, dicentras, epimediums, hellebores, hostas, *Iris foetidissima*, lamiums, tellimas, polygonums, pulmonarias and a host of hardy ferns.

USING CONTAINERS

When planning a challenging garden space, think laterally. Can you use the large blank wall in front of you to support boxes or trough–shaped planters, perhaps arranged in groups or tiers? If you have windows looking onto it at different levels, you might arrange the

boxes directly opposite them. If the wall is part of a neighboring house, you will have to obtain permission for this, and you might also need to hire a professional to carry out the installation. Such high-level planting would also need the special watering device (in the form of an extension lance fitted onto a hosepipe) usually used for hanging baskets and window boxes, and the plant emphasis should be on long-term, easily managed combinations. If a neighbor balks at granting permission, restrict your planting to containers at the bottom of the wall.

Steps to and from a basement level can be used as staging for plants, either by sitting pots on each step, if width allows, or by fixing pots or trough-shaped planters to their sides with brackets. You might plant a climber at the bottom of the steps and train it through railings, perhaps to meet a trailer that is planted at the top.

The roofs of sheds or boiler houses, which are so often found in basements, make excellent places for good-sized planters, provided they are strong enough to support the weight. A box, a barrel or a pot, filled with ivy trained up a pyramid or wigwam makes a decorative feature that is both easy to manage and long-lasting.

LEFT *A bust, framed by ivy and* Lonicera nitida, *draws the eye into the distance.*

FAR LEFT *These steps act as a platform and bring well-filled pots nearer to the light, while the variegated foliage lightens the scene still more.*

more sophisticated affairs might require the help of a professional carpenter. However, garden centers sell ready-made, painted trellis panels in a variety of shapes and sizes. A formal treatment, with a trellis arch and a matching pair of planters sporting standard hollies under-planted with patience plants (*Impatiens*), gives one result; a relaxed grouping of mixed pots and urns against a trellis-backed wall, with *Akebia quinata* (Z 4-9) climbing from a bed at its foot, gives another. Shade-loving ferns grouped against trellis set on a wall form a delicate picture, pleasing all the year; when established, they will seed themselves in every cranny.

LIGHTING THE DARKNESS

Light is the obvious antithesis to dark, and you might want to introduce artificial lighting into your dank space. When you have planned where and how to use the lighting, it is important to call in professional help to install any outside cables and to insure that safety regulations are followed. Remember the general rule that outdoor lighting is best when discreet. A spotlight screwed to a wall, with the switch within easy reach of your viewing position, can be angled to light up the best feature of your tiny garden at night. Alternatively, low spots on spikes, run from an outdoor cable, can be pushed into the soil below shrubs or behind climbers, or tucked in pots, in order to shine gently through the foliage. There are also elegant wall lamps, designed

INSTALLING TRELLIS

Trellis, in all its manifestations, is the antidote to gloom, whether it is white-painted against a plain wall or stained subtle blue-gray, dark green or turquoise against a white wall. It can form arches, be mirror-backed, create false perspectives, hide ugly pipes, support hanging baskets, climbers or trailers, cover a door or mask a storage structure, or even be

ABOVE *Making a tiny garden alluring is vital, and the view from this dark corner is lifted by the brilliant contrasts of light and shade as well as the decorative trellis and paving.*

turned into a small building in its own right. The only limits to this very versatile decorative feature are your imagination and your bank balance.

Simple trellis panels used to support plants are easily fixed by an amateur, but for outdoor rooms, which can be attached to external walls, as you would indoors, their placing part of your overall plan. Storm lamps, such as glass globes sheltering candles, can be placed on a tiny table; they offer a cosy glow and add to the sense of escape that outdoor eating provides.

ESSENTIAL AFTERCARE

Whereas a more open, sunny space can afford a bit of casual disarray, the dank and dark cannot; disorder breeds gloom and must be combated. This does not mean that everything should be cut back ruthlessly – spreading, waving, lush-looking foliage is essential, but the leaves must look clean and healthy, not neglected. Indeed, whatever plants you choose, and in whatever style you arrange them, one of the cardinal rules in a dark area, whenever accessibility allows, is meticulous grooming and hygiene. Keep removing any dead leaves, brushing away rubbish, and spraying dusty plants with water and foliar feed. Plants in small spaces may receive very little light and, as a result, may become etiolated – be ruthless and discard anything past its best, either replacing it with a younger version or trying an alternative.

Pests also, in these difficult positions, have to be treated radically and regularly. It is often possible to remove predators such as slugs and snails by hand in a limited space, and regular sprays of soapy water can daunt aphids, but you may prefer to employ modern chemicals, using sprays to combat aphids and putting down slug and snail poison. When defeat stares you in the face, and a plant succumbs to either the predators or the remedy, whisk it away immediately as ailing plants will only infect those around them. You might try replacing it with an improved species, better able to withstand the harsh conditions.

Since the dank-defeating gardener often has to reach awkward corners, climbing out of windows or struggling through small spaces in order to carry out maintenance, it would perhaps be helpful to choose stylish plants that are more independent. Remember that your initial enthusiasm may wane when faced with too demanding a challenge. The ever-ready *Fatsia japonica*, hollies, bamboos, ivies and aucubas are an ideal choice, not requiring much aftercare. When you have set up suitable plantings and invested in long-distance watering arrangements, you should then sit back and enjoy the results of your efforts.

BELOW *Strikingly handsome hydrangeas bring color to a dark courtyard while bold terracotta pots lead the eye toward the changes of level provided by steps and another area of planting.*

A WATER GARDEN

The tiniest of spaces can incorporate a glimpse of water whether in the form of a fountain or a trickling wall-mask, for example. Here a simple pool, shown in early summer, has been left largely unadorned, apart from a gently bubbling fountain and various decorative pots. The mirror, which is made of glass specially designed for use outside, should be slightly larger than the pool, and adds to the charming effect.

ATTACHING THE MIRROR

Screw wooden battens to the brick wall at approximately 9in intervals, using wider battens at the base so that the mirror will be angled slightly (the difference should only be about 1in over the whole length). Screw a piece of marine ply, which is 1in smaller than the mirror, to the wall battens. Finally, attach the mirror to the marine ply using a special glue, following the manufacturer's instructions carefully. The glue may be obtained from a good glass store. It is important to allow sufficient time for the glue to set.

DIGGING AND LINING THE POOL

Dig the pool out, aiming to create an excavation slightly larger than your finished dimensions, about 14-16in deep and about 8in away from the wall. Smooth the hole thoroughly, removing all large stones and sharp objects. Add a layer of sand about 2-3in thick. Put a heavy-duty plastic or butyl liner in place, and weight it down with bricks on all sides. It is worth investing in a good quality liner, as the cheaper versions often prove unreliable.

CROSS-SECTION OF THE POOL

Install a low-voltage pump to aerate the water and to produce the fountain. It should be raised off the pool bottom to avoid clogging. Employ an electrician to install the outdoor cable that supplies the pump, before laying the paving. Lay the stone paving slabs, cut and laid at random, so that they cover the cable and the liner and slightly overhang the pool edge. (Leave two planting spaces, either side of the mirror, measuring about 12in x 10in for the *Coronilla glauca* 'Variegata.')

MAINTENANCE

• Insure that the pond does not fill with leaves in the autumn. It is also very important to add oxygenating plants such as *Lagarosiphon major* and *Myriophyllum* species, particularly if you intend keeping fish.

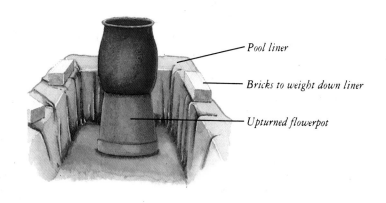

Pool liner

Bricks to weight down liner

Upturned flowerpot

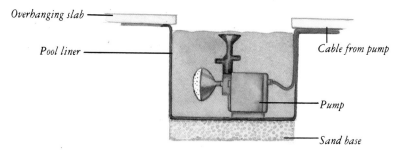

Overhanging slab

Pool liner

Cable from pump

Pump

Sand base

PLANT LIST

On either side of the mirror:
- *Coronilla glauca* 'Variegata' (Z 6-7)

In the two grayish glazed pots:
- *Acer palmatum* Dissectum Atropurpureum (Z 5-8) (left)
- *Hosta sieboldiana* var. *elegans* (Z 3-9) (right)

In the dark blue-glazed pot:
- *Miscanthus sacchariflorus* 'Variegatum' (Z 5-10)

ABOVE *Simple yet stylish, this tiny space uses reflection, moving water and lighting to create a nighttime theater.*

CHAPTER TWO

TRICKS
AND ILLUSIONS

Visual tricks and illusions are a fundamental part of our lives, whether we are choosing clothes or decorating our living spaces. In terms of our outdoor rooms, how much more exciting it is to create a garden of surprises, one whose size may be minuscule but whose vistas seem to abound. Most fun of all is to orchestrate some kind of illusion, a device to suggest that this tiny space is just a taster, while a far larger garden lies beyond. This chapter explores the range of inventive ploys that can be used to make a small space appear larger, from *trompe l'œil* painting (see page 24) to the clever positioning of mirrors, from trelliswork to the creation of false perspectives and boundaries. In addition, water in many guises, groupings of plants or well-filled pots, and the strategic positioning of anything at its peak, play a vital role in this game of deception.

In really small gardens, simple space-enhancing effects are easy to stage, if you follow some basic principles. Arrange your

ABOVE *The eye of the viewer is immediately drawn by this beguiling, white seat before taking in the variety of plant shapes that have been crammed into such a tiny space.*

LEFT *This elegantly harmonious design, with its subtle planting, combines vertical and horizontal accents to make the garden seem larger.*

space so that parts of it are hidden, requiring people to investigate and wander, and presenting a surprise when they do so. An arch or false doorway need only be set a small distance away from a boundary, allowing for a glimpse of a path or a climber-clad wall. A device as simple as positioning a large, spreading plant in a commanding pot in the foreground of a small space, which forces you to look around and behind it to see what else is going on, can create an illusion of greater space. And any rectangular-shaped garden is improved by solid, shrubby planting that is allowed to spill out midway along its length, thus creating a wandering line that breaks up the uniform straightness.

Changing the levels in a small plot is another effective means of suggesting space. A small square space will look larger and more interesting when steps, raised beds, a waist-level pond or sunken paved area are incorporated. For example, build a set of false steps, curved or rounded, against a wall, with a decorative tree or shrub in a handsome pot placed in the center. As a general rule, one or two levels are sufficient for a tiny space, with the plants themselves used to create more height, perhaps mounted on pillars or tripods.

A SPACE BEYOND

One of our strongest instincts is to go through doorways, either in person or in our imagination. This effect can be created by using plant shapes or artefacts, or a combination of both. You could paint a *trompe l'œil* door or a view on an end wall, but if this is beyond your abilities, there are easier options. Try fixing a wrought-iron gate to a wall, back it with a mirror, and overhang the whole with climbers to muddle the edges and make you think there is a passage. A simple archway, installed part-way down your garden, furnished with climbers and with a gently curving pathway through it, will also suggest another area of garden to be explored.

An even more powerful illusion could be achieved at the end of the garden. Clothe the true back wall with a dense, dark-leaved climber, then create a false trellis "wall" a little in front. Grow climbers lightly through the trellis and

RIGHT *These dark, well-clipped hedges, half concealing the statue and backlit by brilliant golden foliage, create a false boundary by suggesting space beyond, and also balance the foliage-fringed pond.*

make a passageway through the center, marked with a pair of crisp standards such as box, *Ligustrum japonicum* (Z 7-9), *Laurus nobilis* (Z 7-9), *Elaeagnus* (Z 7-9) or hollies. The suggestion will be of a garden that continues way beyond the trellis.

You could also try painting a back wall both light and dark, the main part being white, with a narrow, door-sized area, perhaps framed by a clipped evergreen, painted darkest black-green. If you added pots of bright annuals, such as zinnias, felicias, arctotis, gazanias, trailing sweet peas, or pelargoniums, grouped at either side, this too would hint at a passageway to another space.

USING PERSPECTIVE

Perspective is a friend to illusion, and a small space can positively swell if perspective is employed cleverly. Try placing a pair of large, well-filled pots at the beginning of a path, leading away from the house. By slightly obscuring the route the path will take, you have deceived the viewer into thinking that the garden is far larger than it really is. Another clever trick involves planting a pair of small trees at the boundary wall, with an opening between them, and placing a pair of small statues or planted urns on either side, to give the illusion of a glade leading to an open vista.

Narrowing a path, as it retreats, will also make the distance appear greater, and bordering it with progressively smaller edging plants increases the effectiveness of this illusion. Another effect could be achieved by making your path both curve and diminish, becoming narrower as it winds behind a solid shrub, and perhaps ending with a flat, empty pool that reflects the planting behind it. If the length of your space is too limited for a pool, a wall-mounted mask trickling into a bowl could take its place, surrounded with planting. An informal design benefits from off-center features, whereas a more classical scheme requires the water feature to be balanced by a statue or urn placed exactly opposite, for example. At the path's farthest point, create a three-quarter-sized false door, either painted or real, flanked by a pair of miniature standards in pots, to give the illusion of a larger perspective.

LIGHT AND DARK COLORS

A little knowledge of color theory will be a great help to the gardener who intends using illusionistic devices. For example, bright and pale flower colors, with darker leaves behind them, appear closer to the eye, giving the impression of greater space between the two plants. For a truly three-dimensional look, set a pot of white tulips against your darkest evergreen, perhaps with more tulips in other colors around it, and in the evening the groups will appear to move, with the white to the fore, and the other colors retreating.

Similarly, at dusk, dark colors will retreat and pale ones will come forward, so surround your white bench against a back wall with dark foliage, or set a pot,

ABOVE *A simple pedestal brings this bust to exactly the right height, enabling her to preside over the jumble of foliage and flowers below.*

crammed with striped creamy gardener's garters (*Phalaris arundinacea* 'Picta', Z 4-9) or brilliant golden *Hakonechloa macra* 'Aureola,' (Z 4-9) as a halfway marker beside a dark group. Statues, busts or any form of sculpture need foliage through which to peer in all but the most formal of gardens, and if a pale figure can emerge through thick, dark planting, it has far more impact than one sitting in full view.

HARD AND SOFT ELEMENTS

A combination of hard and soft elements, such as artefacts and plants, can form winning illusions. For example, a gazebo or arbor, festooned with bushy climbers such as roses, clematis or solanums, and placed in the middle of a small garden, might form a central square from which four paths radiate. The paths may lead nowhere more exciting than the perimeter walls, but if these are obscured by plants, then the garden boundary will be difficult to define.

Water can also aid illusion. Cascades in miniature can be constructed at angles, each falling into a bowl leading to another bowl, which turns at an angle of 45 degrees. If the bowls are half-hidden by good planting, the effect is of a meandering riverlet ending in a pool, itself surrounded by boulders and bulky plants such as *Gunnera manicata* (Z 7-10) and both pool and plant appear part of a spacious landscape.

Lighting can be exploited for its illusory qualities. Spotlit plants take on a magical quality at night, with silvery tree trunks or a weeping shape silhouetted sharply against an unlit background. Spotlighting a feature or plant at the boundary of your space makes it stand out as if in the far distance, particularly if there is an unlit shape in the foreground. The ideal lighting for a small garden incorporates background spots, placed low and hidden behind thick shrubs, with one or two set at angles to highlight special effects such as a pond, a sculpture, a pretty seat or an arbor. Those who use the garden in the evenings require better path lights than the house-based viewer who regards the night garden as a theater set.

PLANTS TO CREATE ILLUSIONS

Plants can also be used to enhance the impact of a decorative feature. We have all admired the effect of apple trees smothered in climbing roses but, in the truly tiny space, less overwhelming illusions have to be conjured up. For instance, an *Acer negundo* 'Flamingo,' which has been pollarded ruthlessly (its branches cut back to the trunk), will put out fresh pink, cream and soft green

LEFT *These little niches, in any ivy-covered wall, make ideal display cases for ornaments.*

RIGHT *The cleverly positioned mirrors, with their uncluttered lines, are used to reflect the rounded oil jars and spiky planting.*

leaves. It will support the tender yet vigorous *Solanum crispum* 'Glasnevin,' (Z 8-9) provided it is cut back severely in spring, and the soft mauve potato flowers will pour through the decorative leaves of the maple all summer long, creating the effect of a pretty flowering tree. I personally like to grow *Clematis viticella* 'Royal Velours' (Z 3-9) through them both to complete the group. A similar effect can be achieved using a technique copied from Italian gardeners. They sometimes grow decorative ivies, particularly golden-leaved cultivars such as *Hedera helix helix* 'Buttercup,' (Z 6-9) up severely clipped standard bay trees (*Laurus nobilis,* Z 7-9). Kept well under control the effect is of enchanting, golden-stemmed, dark lollipops. Other tricks, which use plants, are all the better for being humorous – a terracotta head, with space in the top for planting, might be crowned with *Festuca ovina glauca* 'Golden Toupée' (Z 4-8) and adorned with tresses of *Rosa* 'Golden Showers' (Z 5-9).

USING TROMPE L'ŒIL

In the true sense of deceiving the eye, *trompe l'œil* is an integral part of all design. In a garden context, we generally use the term to mean painted surfaces, with a deceptive sense of perspective, which extend the real landscape into an imaginary beyond. The main skill in achieving successful *trompe l'œil* is to keep the design simple and the style consistent. If you are pursuing a classical theme, for example, with pillars, false doorways with pediments, niches, balustrades, finials, arches and columns, do not then try to incorporate a cottage garden planting within it.

Although distant landscapes, figures, ruins, or glimpses of water can all play their part, any flowers rambling across the design are usually best if they are real. Indeed, as with all forms of art, *trompe l'œil* is highly subjective: while some people enjoy an austere green garden with brightly colored standard roses painted on a far wall, others prefer a distant Tuscan landscape, in the style of a Ghirlandaio painting, which has real dwarf cypresses and a real stone balustrade, covered in ivy, in the foreground.

The term *trompe l'œil* can be used to describe the more simple technique of enhancing a painted feature with real embellishments. For example, you could surround a painted urn, filled with mixed flowers, with real foliage, or enhance a window, painted on a bare wall, by attaching a real, flower-filled, wall-mounted window box (see page 80). Another stunning idea, and one that I have always hankered after, might involve setting a door, which has stained-glass panels, away from a wall and installing a soft spotlight behind it, so that the colored glass, echoed by nearby planting in identical colors, would glow at night. Alternatively, a stained-glass window, set higher up on a wall, with tendrils of creeper winding around it and lighting behind it, might give the illusion of a Victorian chapel adjoining a tiny patio.

ABOVE *This striking classical statue, peeping through a simple, modern sculpture, draws the eye toward the garden beyond, and gives the garden a greater sense of depth.*

LEFT *A beautifully carved "Green Man" wall fountain merges deceptively with the surrounding abundance of foliage, and adds interest to the plain, boundary wall.*

FAR LEFT *This ravishing* trompe l'œil *painting of distant mountains and summer meadows, glimpsed through a doorway, deceives the onlooker with its clever combination of real and false features.*

A TROMPE L'ŒIL GARDEN

This garden, shown in winter, functions largely as a view, rather than a garden in which to dally. The stylish elegance of the Tuscan landscape mural is enhanced by the real plantings; it gives an illusion of greater space as well as amusing the viewer. The back wall must be smoothly rendered and painted white before painting begins.

BUILDING THE WALL AND PLATFORM

Find the center of the garden by measuring from both side walls. Work out the final width of the retaining walls and the steps, and also the distance between the back wall and the retaining walls.

Prepare the foundation for the retaining walls by digging out a shallow trench to a depth of 6-9in. Fill with concrete, and let harden. Build the walls to a height of 7 bricks, with a top row of half bricks on end.

Lay the paving slabs, cutting them around and butting them against the walls (including the space where the steps are to go), thus creating a paved foundation for the steps.

Build the platform, using hard core, behind the retaining walls to a height of approximately 6in above the paving. Use a board to retain the platform foundations until you are ready to pave the platform, again taking care to butt the slabs against the walls. If necessary, leave a gap against the back wall.

BUILDING THE STEPS

For the lower step, use a row of half bricks at the back and a row of whole bricks in the front. Create the top step, which should be level with the platform, by covering the lower step with a row of whole bricks. If necessary, the steps can be raised a little higher by using extra mortar mix.

CROSS-SECTION THROUGH THE STEPS

The false cypress pots should be at least 14in high. Other suitable plants include *Juniperus communis* 'Compressa' (Z 3-8), *J. scopulorum* 'Skyrocket' (Z 5-8) and *Chamaecyparis lawsoniana* 'Minima Aurea' (Z 5-8).

A view in cross-section showing the construction of the retaining walls, the platform and the steps.

MAINTENANCE

• Incorporate water-retentive granules into the pots of false cypresses.
• Mulch the edging ivies and also the camellias well.
• Replace the tender *Dracaena cincta* 'Tricolor' if it is spreading.
• Keep the topiarized boxwood immaculately clipped, and turned regularly.

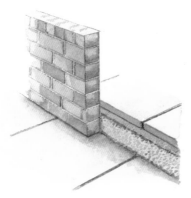

A retaining wall and the platform.

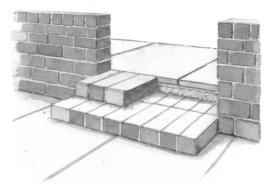

Building the steps.

PLANT LIST

In the foreground:
- A pair of small box topiary spirals
- *Camellia* 'Lady Clare' (Z 7-9)

On the side walls:
- *Hedera helix helix* 'Green Ripple' and *H. helix helix* 'Parsley Crested' (Z 6-9) underplanted with *Hebe rakaiensis* (Z 8-10)

On top of the walls:
- Pots of *Sempervivum tectorum* and *S. arachnoideum* (Z 5-10)

Behind the walls:
- False cypresses

In the central urn:
- *Dracaena cincta* 'Tricolor' (Z 9,10)

A D O R N M E N T S   F O R   T H E   T I N Y   G A R D E N

*J*ust as pictures play a vital role in decorating the walls of our homes, so adornments, such as statues and sculptures, pots and containers and other more unusual ornaments, can enhance our gardens. They are especially useful in the smaller garden plot. In fact, it could almost be said that no tiny space should be without at least one of these features. Italian gardeners, from Roman times to the present day, have always been strong supporters of this view, sitting stone figures among elegant garden designs with a confident touch, and a study of their gardens, old and new, is sure to provide inspiration. It is a good idea to consider such well-executed designs before choosing a statue or a more abstract piece of sculpture for your own garden.

A most important consideration when adding any ornamental feature is to insure that it blends successfully with the style of your garden. This is not at all dependent on the size of the garden. A good statue or urn, for example, does not have to be diminutive just because your garden is tiny.

ABOVE *The technique of setting one sheet of water below another, to create hanging lakes in miniature, is seen in this descending row of bowls.*

LEFT *Small spaces can cheerfully incorporate large, solid ornaments, and the simplicity of these massive vases on pedestals is balanced by the architectural plant shapes.*

Indeed, a large piece of sculpture on a substantial shelf can fit perfectly into a small design, provided you have sufficient room for it and the feature is decorative. I have even seen a full-sized, antique Italian wellhead occupying most of a tiny town garden, but it looked marvelous with roses frothing above it, *Alchemilla mollis* (Z 4-8) at its feet, and just enough room left in the garden for a camellia, a hosta or two and a small *Phormium tenax* (Z 9-10). The simplicity of the wellhead ensured that it could blend into any backdrop, whereas an elaborate, over-decorated figure might have looked foolish.

In the main, ornaments that are large in relation to the size of the garden are most effective. It is always better to have one solid statue, with a single handsome plant beside it, than two or three inferior pieces huddled among a fussy grouping of pots. Even in a tiny garden, a full-sized figure could be placed against a wall, perhaps surrounded by a clipped box hedge and shaded by one small tree, or it could be left alone with a scattering of ivy.

ABOVE *This charming mermaid, carved out of driftwood, combined with the white seashells, creates a maritime theme in this tiny corner.*

RIGHT *These delicate* Argyanthemum *flowers, in beautifully glazed pots, provide a pretty contrast to the pair of lemon trees, whose flowers will scent the entire courtyard.*

climbing the wall and a small, rounded shrub such as a *Hebe rakaiensis* (Z 8-10) planted in a gap left in the paving.

If space is limited, and several ornaments are used, always choose those that will blend well with each other. It is no good trying to include a classical statue in a Japanese-inspired garden, for example.

Extra care should also be taken when mixing old and new features. A simple concrete cube, thickly painted with liquid manure, will soon acquire enough patina to blend with an antique urn, letting you create the height that may be needed for greatest effect. Plants also make excellent additions if you are trying to blend old and new features. In a lushly planted garden, I once admired a beautiful antique stone urn whose base was, in fact, made of molded concrete. The base provided the necessary height to raise the urn, and yet, covered in a clematis that had been trained over wire mesh, it created a handsome ornament, set against an evergreen hedge. The planting within the urn was restricted to silver foliage, a masterpiece of restraint.

A pleasing modern sculpture may be incorporated within any style of planting, but, in general, the simpler the shape and the more natural the material used, the more versatile it will be. In a small space, a handsome piece of stone, positioned with care, becomes an ornament in its own right, and when water trickles over it from a hidden source, it provides a vital focal point. Large stones or boulders can be obtained from water garden retailers, who, stocking material from different parts of the country, offer a variety of shapes and colors. In a small space, it is wise to select gravel, boulders and paving in similar colorings, as too wide a color variation can be unsettling. The stones or boulders can be used in many ways: in a gravel garden, they make excellent edgers, marking the division between plants and paths; and when the stones are arranged in a particular shape, such as a circle or semi-circle, for example they become an unusual garden adornment, both low-key and sympathetic.

POTS AND CONTAINERS

No tiny space could fail to be improved by pots, whether they are empty, crammed with plants, restrained or billowing, used as additional ornaments, or as the only source of planted material. They are infinitely adaptable and can either "lift" a garden by the way they are grouped, provide an impact, or hide a horror. They will let you grow tender or tricky plants, or experiment with color, shape and style. Tall oil jars or Ali Baba pots, with their pleasing and rather sensuous shapes, as well as large trough-shaped planters and urns, are often lovelier left unplanted, forming a natural piece of sculpture in themselves.

Paving and pots share a particular affinity, and a combination of them will form a garden in itself. The smaller the space, the larger part a pot can play. The pot can either be grouped with others to form a well-mixed combination of flowers and foliage, placed in an austerely planted pair to create a more formal effect, or simply used alone and filled with one superb plant. One advantage of using pots is that they can be moved easily, either according to the season or when practical needs dictate.

For example, they can be removed when the space they occupy is needed for outdoor eating, and then returned later for decorative display.

Container-grown arrangements will respond to changing seasons more speedily than a conventional garden border, letting you enjoy each display for longer, if you plan well. Early and late narcissi, for example, can be followed by tulips and, soon afterward, by lilies, while annuals can be potted and used as early summer displays as you wait for your true summer flowers to mature. Fading flowering shrubs that have carried on all season are given a new lease of life when tucked into a pot and offered a new position. Fuchsias are excellent for this, using one- or two-year old plants and putting them in a good-sized container, filled with new compost, in a sunny and sheltered situation. Any pot with a handsome occupant can be popped in front of a dying corner, delaying the onset of winter, and even the dullest space improves when a pot filled with colorful winter pansies is whisked into the foreground.

For a modest outlay of time, effort and money, you can give your tiny space, particularly a courtyard, a prettily planted pot whose effect will be out of all proportion to the initial investment. Container-grown hostas, for example, can nestle out of sight under a bench, coming out to spread their lovely painted leaves in a shaded spot, and returning to

obscurity when either ribboned by slugs or browned by frost. Lifted onto a shelf or put on top of another upturned pot, decorative plantings will bring color and interest as well as adding another dimension to small spaces.

Many plants, such as topiary (a style of embellishment that is becoming increasingly popular), and the exquisite bonsai, actually look better in pots than they do in the ground. Indeed, pots of spring bulbs will lift winter spirits better than any champagne, and generous tubs of highly scented lilies simply epitomize summer.

OBJETS TROUVÉS

If you visit yard sales, you may find more unusual objects, albeit moth-eaten and moldering, which could be turned into wonderful features to adorn your garden. A ship's figurehead, its paint peeling, might be installed against a wall, and a fine mermaid's torso would look splendid emerging shyly through a ruff of ferns. Discarded fairground horses, equally decorative, will also lend themselves very well to a little foliage and fantasy. I have even seen an old dress-maker's dummy rotting gently away behind a tree, crowned with a suitably ancient straw hat! Ornamental birdcages from Eastern countries could hang decoratively from trees, with a pot-grown *Strelitzia* (tender) perched inside. Baskets, in myriad shapes, can be planted and used as adornments, although somewhat short-lived, and modern willow sculptures improve any small garden.

Animal sculptures and statues, in various shapes and sizes, make excellent garden ornaments. Use stylized sculpture such as the magnificent Dogs of Fo (giant, leonine dogs originating from China), which appear in salerooms from time to time, and proud lions guarding balustrades or piers, or try more humdrum pieces such as a humble stone

LEFT Objets trouvés *make unusual adornments, and this stained-glass window and Medusa-like statue enhance a tiny garden.*

RIGHT *This table, surrounded by carefully placed pots, containing foliage plants that blend with the blue-gray doors, forms a perfect platform for potted bonsai.*

FAR RIGHT *The colors of this mosaic pot are reflected by the richly mixed planting.*

DISPLAYING TO BEST EFFECT

Your precious garden ornaments can often become obscured by foliage when placed at ground level. One solution for displaying a group of small figures or a bust, for instance, is to build a waist- or shoulder-height platform on which to sit it, using solid brackets screwed securely into a sound wall. Then plant climbers at the foot of the wall, training them up and pruning them ruthlessly to form a frame around the group. On a shaded wall, use an ivy such as *Hedera helix helix* 'Goldheart,' (Z 5-9), or a well-clipped pyracantha, so that the living shape complements the sculpted one. The same type of platform could hold a large trough-shaped planter, planted with ivies that are trained to hang down wire or twine, thus forming swags of living material, perhaps with neatly clipped box balls at either end.

hedgehog sitting happily on a wall. Whatever style of sculpted animal you choose, take care that the sculpture is realistic and well-carved, and avoid any with human attributes.

Beaches are another prime source of unusual garden ornaments. Boulders and large stones, found on the shore or on rough ground, can be tucked at the feet of any plant, or placed strategically in a bed, or perhaps used to mask a dull pot.

Seashores also provide shells, twisted pieces of sea-silvered wood and glass bottles whose humble origins have been washed away, leaving only bright colors and soft shapes with which to embellish your garden. You could turn a shell collection into a decorative garden feature by placing the shells on a low wall or even making them into a picture. Add a wall-mounted fountain, with a bowl below, and a fern or two, and you have a garden.

The plant material for these ornamental gardens can be as simple or as elaborate as you choose, used either to enhance a sculpture, or to hide the less satisfactory parts of it. Indeed, when the ornament is less than perfect, a shrouding of greenery or a draping of foliage will work wonders. Architectural plants with clean, dramatic lines, such as phormiums, agaves, yuccas, euphorbias, hellebores, bamboos, aralias

BELOW *The blue trellis, silvery onopordums and potted sempervivums create a highly sophisticated color combination.*

and ailanthus will add one dimension. Softer shapes, such as those offered by ivies, *Alchemilla mollis*, ampelopsis, actinidias, vitis, hebes and euonymus will create another. Both container-grown plants and statues, weight permitting, can be moved around to maximize the relationship of ornament to planting.

Using plants to enhance ornaments is also a source of endless fun. Try using a figure with "hair" made of ornamental grass; a terracotta herb pot planted with echeverias; a hedgehog whose body is composed of cress, beloved of children; a lead leaf-shaped bird bath set amongst water lilies in a tiny pond; or a pot of giant blue oat grass (*Helictotrichon sempervirens, Z 4-9*) masquerading as a waterfall.

A more modern look, using abstract shapes in stainless steel, concrete, stone or wood, could be balanced with cacti in a scree bed or in simple pots. Cacti themselves, when well grown, closely resemble sculpture, and you could create a striking landscape, in a sunny courtyard, by combining them with an abstract sculpture.

Many of the most striking sculptures incorporate water, in the form of fountains, trickles, splashes or rills, together providing an extra dimension in the tiny garden. Wall fountains, in the form of spouting masks or dribbling taps, have been with us for a long time, but the improved quality of fiber glass "fakes" has fuelled a demand for small and manageable water-bringers. A fake fountain pouring water over stone, with

the engagingly named *Juncus inflexus* 'Afro' (Z 6-9) twirling its wild green locks from a nearby pot, backed by nodding *Cyperus papyrus* (Z 9-10) or *Carex pendula* (Z 5-9), can create a ravishing garden that will be the envy of those who struggle with patchy lawns and indefatigable weeds. Figures of all types gain tremendous impact when placed with a sheet of still water beneath them. A handsome stone lion, for example, might sit massively on a platform gazing at his own reflection.

DECORATIVE TRELLIS

Trellis has long been used purely for adornment, and medieval paintings depict trellis as part of the geometric patterns so fashionable in the gardens of the period. There are also endless possibilities for using trellis in the garden today: why not build and paint a trellis shape, make a trellis arch and grow a climber over it, put a trellis wigwam on top of a wooden planter and let annual climbers scramble through it, then leave it bare and elegant in the winter?

Treillage, the French term for trellis-based conceits, includes other gloriously complicated and elaborate designs, many of which can be simplified and adapted to a tiny space. A trellis pillar, for example, will provide a beautiful support for a pot of trailing foliage, and its lightness makes it more suitable than a stone pillar for a small garden.

When installing trellis, remember that fairly thin wood can be used for purely

be fixed to sit directly on top of a wall, with supporting posts between each panel running down the wall, or screwed into the wall with two-thirds of the panel showing above the bricks.

If you use trellis to embellish your tiny garden, consider what effect you want to create. If you want a rural look, then unpainted wood is the best choice, but marvelous effects can be achieved through the use of color. Indeed, for a more sophisticated finish, paint or stain the wooden trellis: white will provide extra light in a dark area; soft blue-gray will flatter plants; dark green is smart and crisp; and bright colors would be cheerful on a roof, perhaps, or as part of a modern, color-themed garden.

If you wish to grow climbers, there is a vast range of suitable plants to choose from. Try cultivars of *Clematis macropetala*, *C. alpina* and *C. viticella* (Z 4-9). These are fast-growing, as are annuals such as *Cobaea scandens*, sweet peas, clockvine (*Thunbergia alata*) and morning–glory (*Ipomoea hederacea*). Tender plumbago or *Ampelopsis glandulosa* 'Elegans' (Z 4-9) will also provide some pretty summer color.

Trellis has the added advantage of being a very practical adornment. It can be made into pillars and obelisks to create height, used to create seats or shelves, while trellis buttresses are an elegant and decorative way of hiding a storage area or even ugly pipes. For instance, why not cover a mundane garden shed with elaborate trellis, and turn it into a striking adornment?

ABOVE *The uniform shape of these clipped box balls in stripy pots is echoed by the sophisticated stone finials on top of the garden wall. With the spouting Neptune wall-mask, surrounded by pots of petunias and nicotiana, this striking feature provides a perfect combination of planting and ornament, nature and artifice.*

ornamental purposes, but if you want to grow climbers, a thicker and more solid lumber is necessary. Good, solid panels of treated, unpainted trellis can be bought from builders' merchants and garden centers, or you can build and install the trellis yourself (see page 52). If you are using ready-made panels, they can either

A JAPANESE-STYLE GARDEN

This minuscule garden, shown in spring, is the result of meticulous planning. Before starting work it is important to survey the area from many vantage points, to think about your preferred view, and to take note of the angles of light and shade. These factors will influence where you position the wooden decking, boulders and pebbles, and the plants. Measure the distance between walls, windows and the door carefully, allowing for any intrusive pipes, windowsills or drainage outlets.

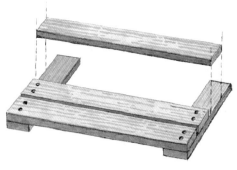

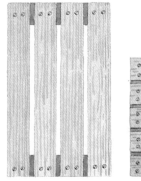

Building the decking.

BUILDING THE DECKING

You can buy decking in ready-made squares from DIY shops and garden centers, so should you distrust your carpentry skills, the design could be fitted around these. Alternatively, buy treated lumber, measuring 4in x 2in and cut it into suitable lengths – perhaps 2ft for so small a space – and sand the ends until they are smooth.

Two lengths form the supports at either end, while the others are laid across them as slats. In this design, the decks are rectangular, so cut shorter lengths for the supports, and use the longer ones to form slats. Using spacers, insure the slats fill the area evenly, fixing them to the supports with two nails at either end. To achieve a more professional finish, use brass or rust-proof screws, countersunk below the surface, filling the holes with wood filler to match the lumber color. Make the decks for the bonsai in the opposite way, with long supports and short slats, in order to provide a contrast in direction.

LAYING THE DECKING

Position the decking carefully, adjusting it to fit your space, and drawing its position on the ground. Raise the level of the decking at the back by 4in and remember to leave enough room for the plants. Prepare a base by firming the ground or subsoil, putting down 3in compacted gravel, and topping it with the same depth of sand. Make the step up particularly firm. When settled, lay the decking in position and cover with old sacks, or newspaper.

ADDING THE DETAILS

Adorn the garden with a mixture of boulders, large pebbles and rocks. These can be found at most garden centers, but beaches are also an excellent source of interesting decorative features, such as gnarled, silver driftwood.

Start to prepare the surrounding earth, adding good compost, and general fertilizer, and incorporating fine grit if the soil is heavy. Place the key plants, still in their pots, and stand back to view the effect. Put in the plants, arranging the boulders lightly around them, and taking care that they are buried slightly to make them part of the scene. Collect the smaller plants, and do the same "look-and-think" routine before planting.

MAINTENANCE

- Remove the spring planting and replace with white patience plants in the summer.
- Brush and groom the plants meticulously, removing ailing leaves or twigs. Water the plants.
- Scrub the decking regularly as the wood can become slippery in wet weather.

PLANTING PLAN

1 *Pinus densiflora* 'Umbraculifera' (Z 5-8)

2 *Azalea* 'Palestrina' (Z 5-8)

3 *Fatsia japonica* (Z 8-10)

4 *Pleioblastus viridistriatus* (Z 8-10)

5 *Chamaecyparis pisifera* 'Plumosa Aurea'
(Z 4-8)

6 *Sisyrinchium striatum* 'Aunt May' (Z 7-8)

7 *Acer palmatum* 'Dissectum' (Z 5-8)

8 *Hosta fortunei* (Z 4-9)

9 *Pinus mugo* 'Gnom' (Z 3-7)

10 Miniature *Narcissus* (mostly Z 3-9),
Primula x *polyantha* (Z 5-7) and *Muscari*
(mostly Z 3-8)

11 *Liriope muscari* and *L. muscari* 'Silvery
Midget' (Z 6-10)

12 *Azalea kiusianum* (Z 6-9)

13 *Euphorbia polychroma* (Z 4-9)

14 Bonsai

CHAPTER FOUR

MAKING
AN ENTRANCE

*E*ntire nations are judged by the entrance to their homes, from palaces to shacks, apartment blocks to floating barges. More people see your front door than ever come inside your home, and your front garden has a permanent audience. Despite this, neglect is rife and while care is lavished on the back garden, entrances are often ignored, front paths abandoned, and the space between house and passer-by treated as little more than a garage forecourt. This state of affairs is sad, almost tragic, if you think of the pleasure to be derived, when driving or walking along a road, from the sight of an array of pretty front gardens stretched out before you. It may be a spring grouping of pale almond blossoms, waving daffodils or brilliant forsythia cheering you on, making you forget overcast skies and cold east winds, the midsummer profusion of roses pouring over a garden wall, or even glimpses of flower-packed window boxes, stylish trough–shaped planters and billowing baskets heartening you as you inch

ABOVE *This cosy sitting area, bedecked with flower-filled hanging baskets, is backed by wooden trellis and overhung by purple clematis.*

LEFT *This wonderfully engaging front garden, filled with exuberant plants, invites the visitor to sit awhile on the bench, or to explore the rest of the garden via the meandering stepping stones.*

through heavy traffic. We have a duty to ourselves, and everyone else, to make some effort to brighten up our window on the world.

First, you need to decide on the most suitable approach for the style and period of your building. While your back garden, however tiny, can be a place for fantasy and escape, the front needs to be in keeping with the neighboring architecture and sur-roundings, not in a spirit of dull con-formity, but arranged with a definite theme, with both the plants and the hard landscaping subject to a firm direction. An elaborate wrought-iron gateway, pineapple-topped pillars, balustrades and finials may look splendid in a book, but, unless your house is grand enough to take them, you should settle for something simpler. Your choice of foliage and flower colors will be limited to some extent by the color of your house materials and that of your front door and windows, and these colors will also have a vital part to play.

Practicalities must take priority over

prettiness. No entrance is a success unless you can get into it, preferably with ease and without being drenched, prickled, or thrown off-course. The path should be sound and wide enough for people to walk up unimpeded, even when rain has flattened the planting on either side. The doorway should be well-lit, and a welcoming air created by the overall style of the front entrance. There may be specific considerations to be addressed before embarking on a design for your front garden. Do you have to incorporate a paved area for vehicles? If you are forced to fill your precious entrance space with an automobile, make your planting sturdy and robust, as few passengers will share your tenderness for your shrubs when it is raining, and they want to get inside the front door. What happens to your garbage cans? If they are kept in the front garden, make sure both you and the garbage collector can reach them easily; neither party will relish climbing through a prickly bush in the darkness of winter. If your family needs to bring bicycles through the front garden, allow enough room to maneuver them safely. Is your entrance down or up steps? Can you fit a container in the porch? Which way does the entrance face, and do you use the front or back of your living space?

These days we should also add security to our list of considerations. In towns and cities it is unwise to create a solid hedge behind which prospective burglars can remain undetected while planning an entrance of their own. Burglar-deterrent

ABOVE *The clear yellow flowers of the superb* Rosa banksia *'Lutea' (Z 6-9) adorn the walls of this house while seasonally filled pots cluster beneath the window.*

LEFT *A sunny, sheltered but minuscule front garden has been filled with beautifully planted containers whose soft colors blend to form a peaceful retreat.*

FAR RIGHT *This tiny front entrance, with its simple wooden gate, is festooned with* Rosa *'Golden Showers' (Z 5-9) in the foreground and laburnam, (Z 5-7) whose cheerful yellow color contrasts so strikingly with the variegated holly and the other foliage.*

lights, turned on by human warmth, greatly improve arrivals in the dark as well as warding off unwanted visitors. They can be tucked neatly into a porch or arranged over a doorway before planting starts. Where decorative pots are concerned, make sure that anything removable is either cemented into place or attached by a chain or a spike to the ground.

ENTRANCE TREATMENTS

All the front gardens I admire share the same basic characteristics. Simplicity is all-important: anything too elaborate, involving twists and turns, too many varieties of plant, and too many different forms of paving, is a mistake. Year-round appeal is vital: attention must be paid to winter-friendly trees or shrubs, however beautiful your summer bedding plants.

Most approaches fall into one of two categories. Usually, you can either plant directly into earth or you have to depend on containers to fill your entrance with interest. Urns, pots and other containers could form your entire front garden, whether they are grouped informally by the front door, or marching in a line or positioned in pairs for a more formal treatment. When using containers, the bulk of the plants should be evergreen, with color as a seasonal accessory to lift your spirits.

If you are planting into earth, think first about aspect. If your garden faces north or east, plan mainly for paving or gravel and choose plants suitable for

shade; do not attempt a lawn. If your entrance garden has a sunny aspect, the range of planting suggestions is wide, but the overall effect still needs to be simple to make the strongest statement. Opt for one major flowering plant in any season, and contrast it with foliage color alone, rather than with more flowers: perhaps a climbing yellow rose for summer, set against the spreading large-leafed perennial, *Tellima grandiflora* 'Purpurea' (Z 4-9) and the slow-growing purple birch, *Betula pendula* 'Purple Splendor' (Z 4-9).

In terms of design, there are many options, depending on the shape of your front entrance space. Where feasible, a

change of level creates interest in a front garden. Keeping the path at one level, you could raise or lower the area beside it by the depth of one brick. You might plant a low hedge beside the path, raise the area beside it, and keep the top of the hedge trimmed to the raised height. If you prefer to step down from the path into a sunken area, you could then create raised beds on the boundary between you and your neighbor's property, or the road. If the front garden faces south or west, you might sink the front garden a little, pave it, plant hedges on both boundaries, and install a seat surrounded by lilies, annual sweet peas (*Lathyrus odoratus*) and roses, making a secret sitting-out area.

Some cottage entrances seem to call for a winding front path or a gentle curve leading to the front door. Remember the temptation of short-cuts, and take care to enhance the curves so they cannot be stepped over, or plant a low, prickly bush to discourage deviation. As a general rule, however, it is best to keep the route to the front door as direct and unobstructed as possible, relying on planting for shape and interest, rather than expecting people to play a game of hopscotch in order to reach you.

PLANTING IDEAS

Restricted planting, combined with simple shapes, suits all but the most countrified of settings. You might have a single camellia or magnolia, set in gravel, with a

neat, low hedge against the road. Or you could choose to have a hedge of golden box, with the gate and front door enhanced by a clipped topiary shape in containers, and thymes wandering in and out of a paved path.

In the tiniest of garden spaces, scale the plants down: raise up a trough-shaped planter by the window so that the plants can be easily appreciated, and plant it with low clumps of dwarf daisies, small hebes, easy alpines and sedums, campanulas, dwarf phloxes, erigerons and violas, with sisyrinchiums, saxifrages and a miniature conifer or two. This would form a simple alpine garden on the flat, with a few paving slabs among the plants to aid clipping and weeding.

I know of a delightful, west-facing front entrance, measuring approximately 10ft square, with a path along one side that

leads to the front door. Beneath the front window the space has been neatly divided into four tiny squares, using bricks to form paths. The center is defined by a circle containing a large, slightly raised, dragon-decorated Thai pot, filled with lilies and trailing pelargoniums in summer, small narcissi and grape hyacinths in spring, and pansies in winter. Each square is treated as a minuscule cottage garden, crammed with purple salvias, rue, thymes, miniature roses, a half-standard patio rose, a standard gooseberry bush, small hebes and dwarf azaleas, silver artemisias and dianthus. All are kept rigorously controlled, with an informal edging of cut-leaved choisya (*Choisya ternata*, Z 8-10) bordering the front railing, and a neatly clipped *Rhamnus alaternus* 'Argenteovariegata' (Z 7-9) marking the next-door boundary. A clematis shares the small bed beside the front door with a rose, balanced on the far side of the bay window by an

LEFT *The soft pink and white flowers in this tiny seaside garden, which is backed by the brilliant blue of a sunlit sea, are a perfect complement to the simple, white gate and clean, wooden decking path.*

FAR LEFT *The overflowing abundance of fuchsias, dianthus, pelargoniums, loniceras and clematis, which surround the door and window of this entrance, and the simple gravel pathway, is a lovely example of a successful cottage garden planting.*

upright rosemary. Feeding, cutting back and replacing the pot's planting three times a year are the only chores, resulting in a decorative, ever-pretty approach.

For a similar style of garden, but facing north, you could create a raised bed against the front wall, backed by a low hedge of golden privet, planted with a *Prunus subhirtella* 'Autumnalis' (Z 4-8) in the center, surrounded by white hydrangeas (*Hydrangea macrophylla* 'Madame Emile Mouillère', Z 6-9). Against the house a sloping arch might support a climbing hydrangea (*Hydrangea*

anomala petiolaris, Z 5-7), forming a cover for garbage cans as it continues up the wall. A clipped variegated holly could mark one side of the bed and a mahonia the other. Continuing the white theme, a large terracotta pot by the front door could hold white flowers – patience plants in summer, white-flowering heathers in winter – and silvery ivy to soften both. This would make a trouble-free garden for a busy person, requiring only annual mulching and clipping.

Many town houses only have a front garden. A formal, disciplined approach

ABOVE *Herb gardens make a superb choice for a sunny entrance, offering scent and texture as well as color. The regularity of the paving, edging bricks and gravel in this front garden is offset by the profusion of plants spilling over the edges of the design.*

would create a spectacular garden that utilizes the entire width of the house. A stone path might lead to the door, with a yew hedge to one side, clipped into a severe wedge, with topiary balls at either end. Edge the other side of the path with a silver box hedge (*Buxus sempervirens* 'Elegantissima,' Z 6-9), which has half-standard clipped balls at intervals along its length. Bring the top of this hedge level with a raised stone-paved area beside it, place an elegant stone urn on a pedestal in the center, and plant the urn with silvery ivies and white flowers. A raised bed, bordering the party wall, and planted with *Choisya ternata* (Z 7-9), might mask an outside garbage can store, and a bed on the front wall could sport a pair of standard box trees, underplanted with skimmias and small variegated vincas. This garden would require minimum upkeep, but such a formal design must be kept crisp and pristine at all times. It is, indeed, very important to insure that its geometric lines do not become blurred.

Many modern developments consist of houses or apartments facing out onto a wide communal entrance. If you do share gardening space, compare other people's approach, and amend any part of your scheme that would be completely unsympathetic to the surrounding designs. If you want to maintain an element of privacy, a columnar conifer, planted against a house wall, makes a strong statement, and indicates the division between one property and another, while hollies are invaluable for preventing short cuts through your space.

When choosing plants for this area, take the aspect of the garden into account. Sturdy evergreens, softened by groups of hardy geraniums, low euonymus, dwarf barberry or bergenias, and epimediums are soothing for a shady entrance. If you have a

sunny aspect, plant *Pittosporum* 'Limelight,' kept trimmed, perhaps underplanted with spreading *Brachyglottis* 'Sunshine' (Z 9-10), *Cotoneaster horizontalis*, with its distinctive fishtail pattern, is another ideal choice, pleasing bees as it climbs up the walls, and underplanted with the small, spiky *Phormium tenax* 'Bronze Baby.'

However, whatever type of entrance garden you decide upon, it may deteriorate quickly if subjected to the daily comings and goings of modern life. If you want to avoid a time-consuming

ABOVE *The formality of the entrance to this elegant town house, with its decorative portico and simple ironwork railings, is achieved through repeated lines of close-set evergreen hedging, while the small standard tree gives the garden added height and shape.*

maintenance routine, which would include sweeping, cutting back, deadheading and an occasional washing-down, opt for a simple design with resilient planting – and enjoy the inviting welcome of a well-kept front garden.

A FRONT GARDEN

The aim of this decorative and relatively trouble-free garden, which is shown in midsummer, is partially to hide the paving slabs by letting the plants creep and spread over them. A pot filled with seasonal bedding plants sits on the slab opposite the window.

The soil requires good preparation. You will need to dig the ground over, and remove any weeds. If the soil is at all heavy, add quantities of compost, peat or peat substitute and fine gravel.

The plants should be positioned in groups of three, five and seven, rather than even numbers. It is possible to avoid a checkerboard effect by arranging the plants in drifts, not solid chunks. They will then flow into one another when fully grown.

When planting the roses, dig large holes, at least 18in away from the wall, on either side of the door, and add well-rotted manure to the bottom, and well-mixed compost and specific fertilizer to the displaced soil that you will then use to backfill the holes. Attach climbing wires to the wall to anchor the roses.

POSITIONING THE SLABS

Position the first two slabs in line with the center of the window. Draw a ring in the earth using two sticks and a length of string, rather like a compass. Alternatively, lay out a length of hose-pipe to form the ring. Then position the remaining four slabs equally around the ring.

LAYING THE SLABS

Dig out the areas for the slabs to a depth of about 5in. Tread the soil firmly, and fill the holes with a light mortar mix of 5 parts sand to 1 part cement. Lay the slabs so that they stand slightly above the soil. Tamp them down with a mallet.

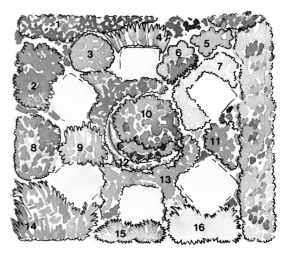

MAINTENANCE

• Remove annual weeds that can pop up in the first few years.

• Check regularly to make sure that the plants do not smother each other.

• Clip the lavender hedge with shears after it has flowered in late summer.

• Remove any dead leaves from the *Bergenia,* and cut off the flowers when they turn brown. Check the clumps regularly for snails.

• Feed the roses in mid-spring with a suitable proprietary fertilizer, and mulch with compost in the autumn.

• Use an all-purpose spray on the roses against aphids, black spot, and mildew.

• After a while, thin the spreaders, particularly if they have become invasive, and pot the surplus plants.

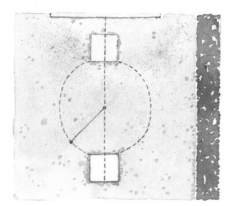

Positioning the slabs.

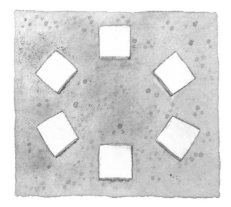

Laying the slabs.

PLANTING PLAN

1 *Rosa* 'LittleWhite Pet' (Z 4-9)
2 *Skimmia* 'Bowles' Dwarf Male' and *S.* 'Bowles' Dwarf Female'(Z 7-9)
3 *Erigeron karvinskianus* (Z 5-8)
4 *Sisyrinchium striatum* (Z 7-8)
5 *Cyclamen coum* 'Album' (Z 5-8)
6 *Erysimum* 'Orange Flame' (Z6-9)
7 *Thymus x citriodorus* 'Aureus' (Z 3-9)
8 *Teucrium chamaedrys* (Z 6-8)
9 *Stachys byzantina* (Z 4-9)
10 *Heliotropium* 'Princess Marina' with

Helichrysum petiolare 'Limelight' and trailing *Verbena* 'Loveliness' (annuals)
11 *Heuchera micrantha* 'Palace Purple' (Z 4-8)
12 *Hebe pinguifolia* 'Pagei' (Z 8-10)
13 *Lysimachia nummularia* (Z 3-8)
14 *Ophiopogon planiscapus* 'Nigrescens' with *Lilium* 'Apollo' (Z 6-10)
15 *Festuca ovina glauca* (Z 4-8)
16 *Carex oshimensis* 'Evergold' (Z 7-9)

On the left-hand side of the path:
• *Lavandula angustifolia* 'Hidcote' (Z 5-9)
Beside the door:
• *Rosa* 'Golden Showers' (Z 5-9) (*left*)
• *Rosa* 'Iceberg' (Z 5-9) (*right*)
On the right-hand side of the path:
• *Bergenia* 'Silberlicht' (Z 3-8) under-planted with *Narcissus* 'February Gold', *N.* 'February Silver' and *N.* 'Tête-à-Tête' (all Z 3-9) in spring.

CHAPTER FIVE

PASSAGEWAYS
AND THROUGHWAYS

*T*he narrow passage, running beside a house and leading to the back garden proper, is all too often ignored, or used as a dumping ground for unwanted deckchairs, wilting house plants, or old barbecues. Enterprising architects and space-hungry families often seize on this spot, build on the party wall, roof it with glass and incorporate it into a kitchen or play-room. If a room leads onto this narrow passage, and a French door can be installed, you immediately gain several precious feet of garden, besides creating a means of circulating when space is at a premium.

However unpromising it looks, there are many ways to transform the dreariest passageway: a coat of paint, trellis against one wall, a wall fountain sited directly across from a house window, or simply the addition of a decorative urn filled with ivy. If storage space is vital and all the junk still has to be accommodated somewhere, build a simple brick structure with a trough–shaped planter on top for plants, or a trellis "house" over which you can grow ivy

ABOVE *This combination of painted mural with decorative trellis, lighting, and soft planting is an ideal way of making the most of a narrow space.*

LEFT *A once neglected passageway has been turned into a pretty garden in its own right. Raised beds have been filled with climbers whose foliage contrasts with the white-painted wall.*

for cover. The structure will not be waterproof, but items can be hidden under it, and the ivy covering it can be kept regularly clipped and controlled.

You might look into the passageway from one end, in which case you have the chance to create a pleasing vista; or from one side, so that you look across to the far wall. Where a window looks down the length of the passage, site a lightweight archway halfway along it, and drape it with manage-able climbers, such as clematis of the *viticella* group, or golden hop (*Humulus lupulus* 'Aureus', Z 4-10), dangling its pretty flowers above your head to frame the view of the garden beyond.

In towns, the floor of this throughway may be entirely covered in concrete, with drains and their covers at intervals along it. Gravel is the answer here. It comes in a variety of sizes and types, so select the gravel according to your personal taste. Immediately the garden space will lighten and look more promising. You need do no more than buy the bags, open them up, and rake the gravel over the concrete base in order to transform an ugly environment into a gentler, more inviting one. The gravel can easily be moved should you require access to a manhole cover; furthermore, gravel is a positive pleasure to brush, and pots of plants will flourish on it.

Where the house window is on the side wall of the passage, think about creating a feature opposite. You might attach an outdoor mirror on the facing wall, angled slightly away from your viewing point to prevent you seeing nothing but your own reflection; surround it by trailing fronds, and install a spotlight to extend the interest into the evening. You might consider fixing painted wooden battens across the mirror to form a false window, then attaching a window box to the base, filled with shade-loving ferns, trailing ivies or patience plants. Where conditions allow, and you have your neighbor's agreement, you could simply site planters along the top of the wall opposite the window, filled with species, such as ivies, clematis, campanulas and *Tolmeia menziesii* (Z 6-8), which will fall down the wall. If the wall is high enough, you could also grow sun-loving species such as helianthemums, arctotis, *Lathyrus latifolius* (Z 6-8), mesembryanthemums or trailing lobelias; as well as upright and trailing pelargoniums and also verbenas.

PRACTICAL SOLUTIONS

The best arrangement for long, narrow throughways is often to build raised beds against one or other of the walls, and fill them with good quality soil. A passage way that leads into an open, south-facing garden might offer a welcome shady area for growing plants that will not tolerate the warm, bright conditions beyond. It would be effective to choose species grown for scent here, planting them in the raised bed, and making sure you leave your window open in summer. *Daphne odora*, and *Sarcococca humilis* (Z 7-9), *Choisya ternata* (Z 7-9) and *Lonicera fragrantissima* (Z 6-8) would all do well in the shade, with *Pittosporum tobira* (Z 8-10) and nepeta in the sun.

Quite often a window, overlooking a gangway, faces a neighbor's identical, mirror-image arrangements. If at all feasible, put a trellis on top of the dividing wall, both for privacy and plants,

LEFT *The change of surface from wooden decking to gravel, combined with subtle lighting and thick foliage plants, makes for an inviting view from garden to house.*

and paint both your wall and the party wall white, possibly building a raised bed against the wall. Since the passage will inevitably be long and thin, a second raised bed farther along, planted with species of varying heights, would help to break up the space. If you were able to dig out a planting space against your own house or the boundary wall, this would enable more climbers to be grown, with low plantings at their feet.

Sometimes the dividing wall between properties rears up to second-floor level, leaving you gazing from your kitchen, or another room, onto a brick cliff. With your neighbor's agreement, trellis could be fixed to the wall to cover it entirely, enabling you to smother the visible wall with a sheet of hardy *Hydrangea anomala petiolaris* (Z 5-7), ivy or Virginia creeper. If you fail to come to a neighborly agreement about fixing anything to the wall, here is an ideal opportunity for a little *trompe l'œil* (see page 24): paint an entire window, complete with scenery, and train your creepers around the edge.

A wider space between houses is more versatile. It might allow you to build a shed of some kind against a wall, in which to store garden chairs and tools; you could stand a good-sized box or planter on its roof, and plant for more color and interest. If your throughway is wide enough, why not turn it into a garden in its own right? Try creating a wandering path along the passage by varying the height and depth of your planting. You might enhance this area

still more by installing a trickling fountain and some subtle lighting, so that the wonderful effect could be enjoyed from all the rooms in the house.

If you have a very sunny garden at the end of your passageway, why not use this shady area for sitting quietly in the cool, or for storing cuttings and seedlings until they are ready for planting. Another excellent idea, along similar lines, is to keep bulbs in pots in this handy space, which are awaiting or recovering from their moment

ABOVE *The airy elegance of this passageway, with its light gravel surface, is enhanced by the topiary underplanted with purple pansies.*

of glory – and even bags of compost can be tucked away here until needed. If, on the other hand, you are lucky enough to have a sunny passageway, why not make it into a wonderful scented tunnel, with roses, clematis, honeysuckles and ceanothus grown over an arch, and a paved walkway below, edged with lavender.

A still more interesting way of transforming an awkward passageway is to build a canal along it. Paying proper attention to construction, of course, consider building a sunken or raised waterway, either with stepping stones at intervals or bridges on which to stand pots of ferns, full moon maple (*Acer japonicum,* Z 6-8) or water-friendly sedges or grasses. Imagine a rill, with jets tumbling into it, or a simple line of water, punctuated by a statue or two, set on brick pillars.

ABOVE *The raised pond, in this elegant passageway, complete with a statue and water lilies, is flanked by pots, simply planted with small bay trees and white petunias.*

I think that this is also an ideal place for a self-contained water feature, subtly spotlit from the house wall, or even a fountain with underwater lighting if you felt really daring. Plenty of light would be needed to turn this awkward space into a night feature: were it to be overlooked from your living room, the splashing water, lit and gleaming, would be a sensational sight. Some narrow passageways are broken halfway along by a projection from an adjoining room, forming a right angle; against this you could try building a false wall to support a wall fountain, again spotlit at night, and with potted ferns at its feet.

PLANTING IDEAS

If you have installed raised beds in your passageway, you will find that shade-tolerant plants, such as camellias, ligustrums, skimmias, bamboos, sarcococcas, *Fatsia japonica* (Z 8-10), aucubas and osmanthus, are the most suitable. Try adding climbers, such as *Akebias,* hydrangeas, ivies and Virginia creeper for height, and then spike the beds with ever-tolerant warf begonias and patience plants for summer color.

If you do not wish to build raised beds, you could excavate a strip of earth along the wall and grow *Fatsia japonica* or *Clematis armandii* (Z 7-9), or simply rely on containers to provide added interest. A plant enthusiast might cram pots and boxes onto every available surface, planting for climbing, softening, cheering or embellishing, while a busy person might settle for a shapely, container-grown camellia or neat standard *Prunus lusitanica* (Z 7-9). There are a vast array of container shapes available now, which lend themselves perfectly to use in narrow passageways and throughways.

The Victorian-style jardinières and wirework stands, which have one flat and one curving side, are simply made to stand against a wall, crammed with ferns and accompanied by fern-filled hanging baskets. Terracotta pots, shaped like wedges of cheese, can be tucked into the angles of walls and planted with a honeysuckle, while the tall chimney pots, found in builders' yards and planted with brilliant begonias, will cheer up a dark, gloomy space.

Country or village throughways may in fact be passageways, leading from a road to a side door, possibly used as a front door. This makes it into an entrance, but the narrowness, and often shade, is a restricting factor when it comes to planting. In such a position, solid evergreen planting in the strip of earth bordering the house wall, of, for example, a bergenia, a hypericum or perhaps *Liriope muscari* (Z 6-10), with a camellia beside the door, would be both soothing and welcoming. Wider spaces might also accommodate a fuchsia or hydrangea hedge, with seaside valerian (*Valeriana,* Z 5-8) arranged elegantly in the cracks between the paving stones. A sunny passage, on the other hand, could support an aromatic rosemary hedge (*Rosmarinus officinalis,* Z 7-9), which will brush against your visitors and cheer them with its delightful scent.

RIGHT *This passageway, half water and half walkway, provides a precious area in which shade-loving plants can be grown as well as a welcome retreat from the sunny garden beyond.*

A NARROW SIDE PASSAGE

Many houses have a narrow side passage, bounded by a brick wall or a neighboring building. This rather dull, claustrophobic area can, however, be transformed into a stylish garden if you exploit the vertical dimension. Indeed, rather than simply concentrating on the ground-based containers to add interest to this tiny space, you should regard the brick cliff as a fernery, and build a striking trellis framework. The trellis produces a pretty effect, fading gently as time goes by, and acts as both a backdrop and a support for the fern-filled pots. The aim is to create a living wall of all shades of foliage, which almost obliterates the trellis.

FIXING THE VERTICAL BATTENS

Measure the area of wall so that you can calculate the number of battens you will need. The battens, measuring 1½in wide and ¾in deep, should be treated all over with dark green wood preservative before being erected.

Screw all the vertical battens into position, using wall plugs. It is important to insure that the screws are a little way in from the ends, in order to leave enough room for putting in the horizontal battens.

FIXING THE HORIZONTAL BATTENS

Nail the horizontal battens to the vertical battens where they cross, forming 12in squares. This will leave enough space for the fern pots. The top rail, and any of the other rails from which you intend to hang pots, should also be plugged and screwed into the wall through alternate vertical battens. Make all the joins as you go along, and take care that they occur at random.

FIXING THE POTS

Hang the flat-backed terracotta pots by measuring the position of the holes in the back very carefully, and deciding where the pot is to go. Use an empty pot to position all your screws. Plug the wall first, and then insert long screws into the plugs. The screws will support the pots easily, providing they protrude from the wall and are angled slightly upward.

Make dull green plastic pots (with a diameter of at least 10 or 12in) into hanging pots by clipping on tripods which have a hook at the end. Hang them, when planted with ferns, at intervals along the top rail of trellis. Here, some small-leaved ivies have also been added to the top row of pots.

Fixing the vertical battens.

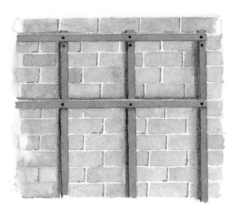

Fixing the horizontal battens.

Fixing the pots.

LEFT *These cup-and-saucer vines* (Cobaea scandens), *planted in blue-glazed pots, have yellow-green flowers that turn purple with age. Here they gently frame the brick archway leading to the garden beyond.*

PLANT LIST

In the flat-backed and hanging pots, ferns such as:
- *Asplenium trichomanes* Incisum Group (Z 5-8)
- *Asplenium scolopendrium* (Z 5-9)
- *Polypodium vulgare* (Z 5-8)
- *Athyrium filix-femina* 'Frizelliae' (Z 3-8)
- *Athyrium niponicum* 'Pictum' (Z 3-8)
- *Polystichum setiferum* 'Divisilobum' (Z 6-9)
- *Polystichum setiferum* 'Congestum' (Z 6-9)

In the large terracotta pots:
- A row of standard fuchsias, all of one variety, and of more or less identical height. (You can use varied heights and colors to create a more casual effect.) Choose fairly hardy cultivars of *Fuchsia magellanica* (Z 7-10) such as 'Maiden's Blush,' or 'Primula'; also F. *microphyllus* 'Isis' (Z 7-10).

MAINTENANCE

- After cutting back the old fronds, add a small amount of fish emulsion or a liquid fertilizer such as Schultz's, to the pots of ferns in spring.
- Water ferns and fuchsias regularly.
- Apply a diluted liquid feed once every two weeks to the fuchsias when the flowers have arrived.

S U N K E N
G A R D E N S

*T*o anyone who struggles, year after year, with a dark, dank space, so sunken or so overshadowed by enclosing buildings that daylight seems hardly to penetrate, the notion that a sunken garden could be regarded as an asset and a challenge, rather than a problem, will defy belief. But there is plenty of scope for improvement and invention, and indeed a garden that is always looked down on, rather than full on, can have its own particular advantages.

Frequently, the sunken garden is a backyard or front garden at basement level, with a flight of steps down into it, which is often overlooked by a window. Here, the challenge is to try and raise some of the plants nearer to the light, without blocking the steps entirely. Brackets to hold pots or planters can be fixed to the outer edge of steps or railings, forming a parallel set of flowery boxes, filled with massed fuchsias, begonias, violas, creeping jenny (*Lysimachia nummularia,* Z 3-8) or ferns. Brackets can also be attached to the walls to hold larger planters, or boxes

ABOVE *The young eucalyptus in the corner of this sunken garden, planted with shade-loving* Fatsia japonica *and* Aucuba, *climbs toward the light, waving its silvery leaves against the walls.*

LEFT *A natural-looking pool, with tree trunk-shaped stepping stones, is an imaginative way of transforming a minuscule sunken area.*

filled with trailing, as well as upward-looking, plants – again the aim is to bring them nearer to the distant sky. Then at ground level, create platforms from anything you can think of: upturned pots, ancient tables, strong wooden boxes or piles of bricks. Position these against the wall, perhaps in tiers, and use them to support planters and pots for your most decorative plants. By including a few trailing plants in your planting scheme you will insure that your makeshift platforms are well hidden.

It is impossible to over-emphasize the importance of good soil when dealing with small spaces. Very few plants enjoy having their feet rooted in badly drained soil, nor do they spring into action when confronted with sterile dust. Almost without exception, any soil in a sunken area will be in poor condition: sour, soggy and lacking in nutrients. Before embarking on any planting, remove as much of the existing soil as possible, digging down as deeply as you can, checking for ancient bed springs, old cans and

ABOVE *The bright cans and pots adorning the walls of this Mediterranean sunken courtyard are filled with colorful pelargoniums.*

mountains of broken crockery. Bag it all up and take it away, then invest in good-quality compost, topped up with farmyard manure, spent hops or other organic materials.

If your sunken garden is surrounded by walls, the foundations may interfere with deep digging, and your spade may bang into debris. Use a pick to remove as much loose material as possible, before putting in the manure, followed by new all-purpose compost or best garden soil, topped up with a mixed organic fertilizer such as alfalfa or Gro-Pro. If the soil is soggy, add soil-lightening granules, while if digging produces a solid layer of clay, break up what you can, and throw in a

thick layer of gravel before the manure. If your soil is fine and dry, remove a good few bags of it, before adding soil mixed with peat-substitute or peat.

CLOTHING THE WALLS

Festooning your walls with colorful plants can be a particularly effective way of cheering up a sunken area. If you have some earth at ground level, concentrate on creating a background for your decorative mixtures, making sure you improve the soil thoroughly before planting. Strong-growing hardy climbers with good clothing properties include: ivies, *Clematis montana, C. armandii, Hydrangea anomala petiolaris, Lonicera japonica* and even *Rosa* 'Madame Grégoire Staechelin.' Put in a few shade-loving evergreens, such as osmanthus, *Leucothoë*

fontanesiana (Z 6-9), *Mahonia aquifolium* (Z 5-8) or *Prunus laurocerasus* (Z 7-9). Stand one or two chimney pots or upturned boxes among them to support a larger, mixed plant group, and add a fringe of shade-tolerant, low-growing shrubs. You will then have a three-tier garden of foliage and flowers to delight the viewer.

Sometimes the view from a window consists of a gloomy well, clad with shiny wall tiles. These can be painted easily, provided you can reach them, using the textured masonry paint specially designed for outdoor use. If the well is part of a shared building, problems may arise, but where it is freely available, you could build a false floor to support pots and planters (see page 62). A less ambitious approach would involve painting the wall and fixing brackets on it to support hanging baskets. Make sure, however, that the baskets are reachable for watering, either by putting them on a pulley system or by using a long-armed watering device. A climber, planted at the foot of the wall, can be trained to wander around the baskets, and the view becomes a source of joy rather than depression.

CONTAINER COMPOSITIONS

An awkward, neglected space below a window requires both agility and determination in order to reach it for planting and watering. One solution is to raise the level of the feature by using an old garden table to support a large but lightweight tub or box. Fill the tub with good compost, and treat it like an outdoor vase, removing anything that flags, and replacing it with new displays. Large, plastic planters are suitable here as they are light but invisible when viewed from above. Choose bold and long-lasting plants, more for their foliage than their flowers, such as *Aucuba japonica* 'Variegata,' with *Euonymus fortunei* 'Emerald Gaiety,' several *Helleborus foetidus*, with *Vinca minor*

and lysimachias to trail, perhaps a good-sized golden privet in the background, and some *Anemone* x *hybrida* 'Honorine Jobert' to throw up their simple, rounded white flowers in late summer. Your planter should be at least 2ft in diameter and 18-20in deep; you could cheat a little by leaving space in the foreground to tuck a large, forced florist's hydrangea. Kept well watered, they flower over

several months, and can be left in position to flower next year or moved to a larger space, where they will increase rapidly.

Such a space would be a perfect candidate for the ingenious "towers" of

BELOW *This welcoming city garden combines cool white planting in a variety of pots and urns with a host of fascinating adornments.*

hanging baskets created by two tiers of metal baskets suspended from a solid stand, and watered by hosepipe from a window above. When the baskets are fully planted with well-fed, spreading annuals, the effect is of a giant bell of flowers and foliage. If your sunken garden is short of light, consider planting ferns and small ivies, with a patience plant or two if you crave color, or simply a huge billowing mass of mixed patience plants on their own. The stand would have to be turned from time to time to produce balanced growth, but even if practicalities prevented you from doing this, the side you see from your viewpoint would look magnificent.

Wide, shallow bowls on a stand, made from either terracotta or a stone composite, are also very useful in a sunken garden. The raised bowl on the classical pedestal means that the plants are nearer the light, and can spread widely and trail down over the rim. In a wide area, a pair, or even three or four such arrangements, set at regular intervals, forms a stylish garden without any additions. Think of a statue, a piece of sculpture, a water feature or a decorative plaque as a focal point with a matching pair of planted containers on a stand at either side. With enough sun, the splendid bedding plant *Scaevola aemula* would fit the bill perfectly: its mauve-blue flowers carry on throughout the summer and the plant appears to climb as it forms circular tiers, spreading and drooping gracefully. Another bedding plant, *Felicia amelloides* 'Santa Anita' or perhaps its variegated version, would offer the same length of flowering, and it also has the added bonus of gracefully upturned tips to its trails.

PLANTS FOR SCENT

A lower garden space should ideally provide luscious scents to waft through your upper window. So it is important to include in our selection those aromatic plants that do well in restricted light. Ravishing *Nicotiana sylvestris*, the tall tobacco plant, grown as an annual, has great, pointed trumpets of sweetly smelling white flowers; *Clematis montana rubens* 'Odorata' (Z 6-9) produces its vanilla-scented flowers in summer. *C. maximowicziana* (Z 5-9) or sweet autumn clematis bears fragrant white flowers in late summer. *Daphne pontica* (Z 7-9) has a delicious smell at night; *Mahonia aquifolium* (Z 5-8), *M. japonica* (Z 6-8) and hybrids of this species all produce yellow, lily-of-the-valley-scented flowers in spring, and lily-of-the-valley itself (*Convallaria majalis*, Z 4-9), tucked into a corner of the paving, will waft its magic perfume through any window. The modest little shrub,

RIGHT *The walls of this sunken area have been decorated with well-planted window boxes and billowing hanging baskets, while flower-filled pots march inexorably down the steps.*

LEFT *Every inch of space in this shady corner has been used, with clematis, honeysuckle and ivy climbing the walls, while the flowerbed below has been crammed full with plants.*

sarcococca, will also astonish you with its powerfully sweet scent in early spring. Honeysuckle smells delectable, and the shade-tolerant roses, *Rosa* 'Madame Grégoire Staechelin,' 'New Dawn,' 'Gloire de Dijon' and 'Parkdirektor Riggers,' for example, all add scent to their other many charms (all Z 5-9).

ALTERNATIVE SCENARIOS

Using fewer plants, or even none at all, is another way of coping with a sunken area. Pave the garden attractively, then set a single tree in the center; it would need to be something pretty in itself, such as a *Parrotia persica* (Z 4-8), a redbud tree (*Cercis canadensis*, Z 5-9) or perhaps a *Gleditsia triacanthos* 'Sunburst'(Z 4-9). In a sunny courtyard, over looked by windows, the glorious *Aralia*

elata 'Variegata' (Z 6-9) would create a stunning effect; it stretches its delicate, finely cut leaves like a wide umbrella, emerging from a twisted walking stick in spring, and is far better appreciated from above.

If your view includes a wall and an area wide enough to move in (over 3ft square, say), you might consider building steps against the far wall, as a stage on which to display your flowering performers. Simple, square steps can be attempted by most DIY enthusiasts, but

RIGHT *Cleverly placed trellis, covered with honeysuckle and ivy, has turned an overlooked patio into a secret sitting area.*

BELOW *This sunken garden, with its simple wooden decking, outdoor lighting and well-planted pots, is a perfect city retreat.*

rounded ones may need a little more building experience or even professional help. The top step might hold a container for a climber, with the middle one, if there were three tiers, supporting pots of flowers grown for color, and the lower one trailers. If there were only two steps, why not place a rustling bamboo in a deep pot on the top step, and several pots, containing a spread of evergreen ferns or hostas, at the bottom. In a restricted space, it would be most effective to have tiny steps ending in a miniature mirrored arch. The arch could be framed with creepers, and the steps lined with miniature plants, such as dwarf hostas, tiny conifers and fairy grasses, marching downward.

The term sunken garden can apply to a ground-level plot that you live above, or one whose intricacy is best appreciated from above. The elaborate parterres so fashionable in Elizabethan gardens were specifically intended to be viewed from above by promenading courtiers. If your window looks downward, and space allows, design an elegant knot garden, featuring your initials, a heart, a Maltese cross, a favorite piece of geometry, or just a simple square with a central urn, planted with dwarf box and filled with gravel. A plain box-edged circle looks stunning planted with patience plants in summer, and primroses and narcissi in spring, or perhaps discreetly elegant planted with a camellia in the center and infilled with *Pachysandra terminalis* 'Variegata' (Z 4-9), a perennial that flowers in early summer.

A KITCHEN WINDOW GARDEN

This striking design, shown in summer, utilizes the well that often exists between two buildings. The walls of the well have been painted white first in order to lighten the whole area, and also to provide an appropriate backdrop for displaying the abundance of thick foliage plants. The false wooden floor supports a variety of well-planted pots and containers, including an old chimney pot, and raises the level of the garden so that it can be viewed easily from the kitchen window. Remember that you may need your neighbor's permission first.

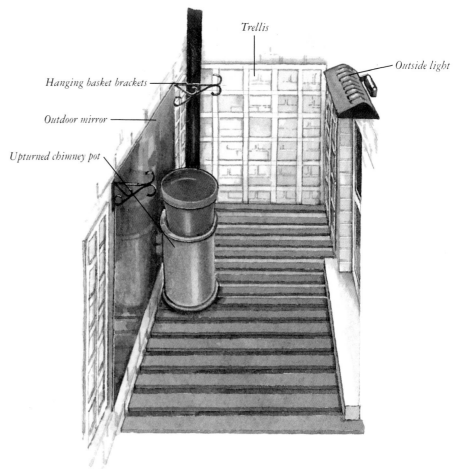

Trellis

Outside light

Hanging basket brackets

Outdoor mirror

Upturned chimney pot

BUILDING THE FALSE FLOOR

Screw two angle irons into the opposite walls of the well. The angle irons should have holes drilled into them every 6in in

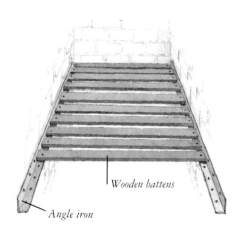

Wooden battens

Angle iron

one angle, and every 3in in the other. Bolt the first side of the angle iron to the wall with high-strength barbed bolts. Using wooden battens, measuring 3in x 2in, which have been stained green with wood preservative, build the false floor just below the level of the window sill by screwing the battens, from below, to the other side of the angle irons.

ADDING THE DETAILS

Screw an outdoor mirror to the wall, exactly opposite the window. Fix white-painted trellis all around the walls to the height of the window. Attach hanging basket brackets on either side of the mirror, so that, when flower-filled, they can be seen from the window.

PLANT LIST

Climbers on trellis:
- *Hedera helix helix* 'Goldheart' (Z 5-9) (on each side of the mirror)
- *Hedera helix helix* 'Green Ripple' (Z 5-9)

In the hanging baskets:
- Fuchsias underplanted with *Hedera helix helix* 'Jubilee' (Z 5-9)

Plain, terracotta pots (underplanted with vincas, ivies and ferns):
- *Camellia japonica* 'Alba Simplex' (Z 7-8)
- *Skimmia japonica* 'Rubella' (Z 7-8)
- *Euonymus fortunei* 'Emerald 'n' Gold' (Z 5-9)
- *Aucuba japonica* 'Variegata' (Z 6-8)
- *Ligustrum lucidum* 'Aureovariegatum' (Z 8-10)
- *Fatsia japonica* (Z 8-10)
- *Aucuba japonica* 'Speckles' (Z 6-9)
- *Impatiens* (annual)
- *Nandina domestica* (Z 6-9)
- *Camellia x williamsii* 'Coppelia Alba' (Z 7-9)
- X *Fatshedera lizei* (Z 7-9)

MAINTENANCE

- Water regularly.
- Spray the plants with a systemic insecticide containing primicarb.
- Prune the plants back in the spring if they become attenuated.
- During the summer, feed the plants with liquid all-purpose fertilizer at monthly intervals.

CHAPTER SEVEN

TINY BACK GARDENS AND BACKYARDS

*E*verything is on show in a limited space, and so it has to be both' better planned and more carefully maintained than a larger garden, which can include seasonal pictures, sweeps of color, whole beds of one species, and dozens of vistas. Our small spaces, however, must combine all the virtues of good gardening, but allow none of the extravagances; over-ambition can be fatal. Aspect is extremely important, and neighboring buildings, trees, or sightlines must always be taken into account when planning a small space.

There is no doubt that the first sight of a neglected small back garden can be daunting. It may have nothing but a dirty wall; it may sport builders' rubble and junk; there may be grass as high as your rake or a forest of self-sown trees. The first priority is to decide on the style of garden to which your life is suited, not vice versa. Clients ask for all-white gardens, lawns, alpines, or billowing masses of climbers; shrubs and flowers, when in fact their garden is north-facing or totally over-

ABOVE *The color of this stone lion wall fountain, echoed by the white patience plants below, provides a gleaming focal point on the ivy-covered wall.*

LEFT *This tiny balcony, with its assortment of terracotta pots, is an excellent vantage point from which to view the splendid paved garden spread below.*

shadowed; or they demand herbaceous borders and old-fashioned roses for a space only 20ft x 20ft. Moreover, it frequently transpires that they are terribly busy and often away weekends. Your garden requirements and your own lifestyle must dictate your planting. Only choose to create something that you can deal with, either yourself or by paying someone else to do so. A grandiose, but neglected scheme, is both a sad sight and a waste of effort.

When planning your back garden, it is important to ask yourself a few basic questions. What do you want from your garden? Do you intend to sit in it, grow vegetables, hang the washing out, play with the dog, make a climbing frame for your children, or just look at it through a window? All successful garden design is based on being selective, on choosing the right style to suit the site, the best plants to grow within it, and the shape in which it will all flourish. Here are some of the priorities that people often list for their ideal garden: privacy; all-year-round

viewing; easily managed but still stylish; a profusion of summer color and scent; a water feature; an attractive view from the windows; and good hard-landscaping, with interesting planting.

A PRIVATE SPACE

One of the most common requirements when creating a garden is privacy. If you want to create a secluded garden, first inspect the area carefully, preferably in winter, and decide how much height you need to add to your existing boundaries. When deciding how to block out an unlovely view, consider using a trellis, a trellis above a wall, a wall proper or a fence, or climbers.

The most economical solution is to put trellis on top of an existing wall, but should you be faced with wobbling boundaries or no boundaries at all, more drastic and expensive measures are called for. If your budget does not stretch to a fence and trellis all the way around, use it to screen the worst view, and use shrubs or small trees for the rest.

If your garden faces north or is so masked by buildings that the only sunny spot is away from the house, and thus more exposed, a trellis-covered shelter or gazebo, containing a hidden seating area, will offer privacy when you are out in the garden. An arch, well-planted to supply both shade and scent, would also afford shelter and privacy when placed over a seat; or it could be set in the foreground particularly to mask an ugly building in the distance.

ABOVE *At first glance there may seem to be too many surfaces in this small area, but the mixture of paving and wooden decking bring balance and elegance to the garden.*

LEFT *The contrast between these white rounded stones and the square paving creates a striking effect, while the color of the tiles is echoed by the bright berries of* Nandina domestica *(Z 6-9).*

RIGHT *This secluded back garden, with its well-worn brick path leading to a cool green lawn and glimpses of color, has an enticing atmosphere.*

Hedges, even if composed of two or three shrubs, can form a private corner, and a weeping tree makes a splendid secret bower. It is unlikely you will sit outside for long in mid-winter, so a deciduous tree, such as weeping silver pear (*Pyrus salicifolia* 'Pendula,' Z 5-7), can be trained to provide a shelter, as can a weeping silver birch, prunus, laburnums or small willows (*Salix*). If you live on the West Coast, consider a ceanothus arbor, or a pittosporum, kept clipped to form a slightly concave seat. Bamboos will also form effective sheltering clumps, but have a tendency to outgrow their welcome. The same is true of the brilliant, fast-growing *Robinia pseudoacacia* 'Frisia' (Z 3-8), whose elegant, dangling foliage will form a secret corner.

SHAPES AND SURFACES

Having established some privacy, your next step is to decide on the shape of your garden. This will be dictated partly by the shape of the plot itself. If it is long and thin, do you break it up, and, if so, by planting or by hard landscaping? If it is short and square, should you impose a curve or circle upon it, or divide it into classic segments? What paths do you need, leading where and why? However short the path, it should always reward the stroller by leading to something, no matter how simple, such as a special plant, a pot, a tree or a piece of sculpture.

A change of level is always an asset, particularly in a limited space. For

example, raising a line of paving by one brick, or marching a line of pots up shallow steps, will help to create a sense of space. The simplest way of suggesting height is to sit a well-planted pot on a platform, or even on an upturned pot, which is kept half-hidden amongst lower plants. Alternatively, attach a slab with brackets to your back wall, and use it to support a pot planted with a conifer or another evergreen, which can then pretend to be far taller than it really is.

The type of surface you choose will help to create a certain mood. A tiny grass lawn, provided it gets enough light to grow well, can turn a miniature back garden into a green oasis with sympathetic planting, or can form a sophisticated pattern among stone or gravel, with equal success. Although the softness of grass has universal appeal, it is important to remember that a lawn requires careful maintenance. Gardeners, particularly those who are new to the restrictions of town gardening, should be aware of its mud-forming tendency, its vulnerability to moss- and weed-infestation, as well as the need to keep it well-trimmed if it is to resemble the glorious green pictured in books.

Hard surfaces, such as stone, brick, gravel, manmade paving, paviours, slate or even wood, all have their devotees, but

LEFT *The combination of raked gravel, carefully chosen stones, and severely restricted planting, in this Japanese garden, makes for a harmonious and refreshing whole.*

the choice you make will depend on your budget. Gravel is the cheapest form of ground cover, and the most versatile, although it is uncomfortable to sit and walk on. Brick is also extremely versatile, and flexible enough to fit round any shape, the small scale of the units making it particularly suitable for tiny spaces. Brick can be combined with manmade paviours to break up, and add interest to, an otherwise bland-looking area. Local stone, although expensive, is unbeatable for lending elegance to the garden as it forms a natural-looking, harmonious backdrop to plants and containers. It is flexible too, since larger slabs can be cut to fit, and looks particularly effective around a pond.

A LOW-MAINTENANCE DESIGN

A garden that can be managed easily by busy people must, inevitably, include a preponderance of shrubs and good, well-laid paving or gravel. Against walls or trellis, avoid climbers, which entail too much tieing back, pruning and general management, and use only wall shrubs and pillar roses. Incorporate a larger than usual number of evergreens, including some variegated cultivars, as well as those with golden or purple leaves. Concentrate on low-growing edging plants, including those with silver foliage such as lavender, *Artemisia* 'Powis Castle' (Z 5-8), *Hebe albicans* (Z 7-10), or *Stachys byzantina*, to complete the picture, so that both color and interest are provided throughout the

year. If you want to enjoy seasonal displays, plant up containers with your favorite plants, removing or replacing them once they are past their best.

BUILT-IN FLEXIBILITY

You will find that a number of seemingly permanent garden structures can be transformed into something else when they are no longer needed for their original purpose. Such flexibility comes with forward planning. For example, while crawling babies prefer grass, toddlers' tricycles and wheeled toys need

ABOVE *This simply planted and restrained back garden is an ideal spot for sitting peacefully in the shade, and an excellent antidote to city frazzle.*

a paved expanse, so one must give way to the other. A circular, brick-edged sandpit can be converted into a round pond, a scree bed for alpines or an Italian-style home for terracotta-potted standard shrubs trained into a "lollipop" shape. A children's swing, set in concrete, could be transformed into an unusual support for hanging baskets and twining climbers, or into a stand for a garden hammock, and a lawn that has been ravaged by bat and

A LOW-MAINTENANCE GARDEN

This garden is ideal for those with a busy lifestyle who do not place gardening high on their list of priorities, but still enjoy pleasing surroundings. It provides a perfect space for outdoor eating, entertaining, and relaxation, particularly in the summer.

You may employ a professional to carry out the heavy construction work, or you may prefer to undertake the challenge yourself; either way, the final garden will need little maintenance.

CONSTRUCTING THE RAISED CORNER BEDS AND SEATING WALLS

Prepare the foundation for the raised corner beds by digging out a 2ft x 2ft square to a depth of 9-12in, and filling with concrete. Build the retaining walls for the corner beds to a height of 6

Building the corner beds and seating walls.

bricks, topped with a row of bricks on edge, making the wall a total of 7 bricks high.

Lay a slightly smaller depth of foundation for the internal support wall (against the left-hand boundary) of the seating bench. Use hard bricks for this wall so that the construction is strong enough to support the seating slabs.

Lay paving slabs over the whole area on a layer of sand and cement mix, having leveled the garden well first. Insure you butt the slabs up to the walls.

Finally, build the front wall of the seating bench directly onto the paving slabs to a height of 5 bricks, so that it butts against the corner bed. Infill the seating bench with a strong cement mix containing broken bricks. Lay paving slabs on top of the walls to form the seat.

PLANT LIST

In the right-hand border (from top to bottom):

- *Fremontodendron mexicanum* (Z 9-10)
- *Carex oshimensis* 'Evergold' (Z 7-9)
- *Rosmarinus* 'Miss Jessopp's Upright' (Z 7-9)
- *Choisya ternata* 'Sundance' (Z 7-9)
- *Ruta graveolens* 'Jackman's Blue' (Z 5-8)
- *Ceanothus* 'Yankee Point' (Z 7-10)
- *Phormium cookianum* 'Cream Delight' (Z 9-10)
- *Festuca ovina glauca* (Z 4-8)
- *Rhamnus alaternus* 'Argenteo-variegatus' (Z 7-10)
- *Lonicera nitida* 'Baggesen's Gold' (Z 6-8)

- *Viburnum tinus* 'Variegatum' (Z 7-8)
- *Euonymus fortunei* 'Emerald Gaiety' (Z 5-8)

In the raised corner beds:

- *Camellia japonica* 'White Swan' (Z 7-8)

On the back wall:

- *Hedera helix helix* 'Buttercup' (Z 6-9) with *Alchemilla mollis* (Z 4-8)

On the right-hand wall:

- *Trachelospermum jasminoides* 'Variegatum' (Z 8-10)
- *Hedera helix helix* 'Goldheart' (Z 6-9)

PLAN VIEW AFTER BUILDING

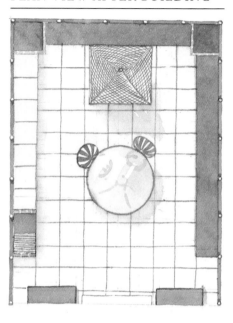

This plan view of the garden shows the French doors and chests for storing the striped cushions.

MAINTENANCE

• Sweep the paving and occasionally cut back any invasive plants.

• Regularly water the plants, unless you have installed an automatic watering system.

• Plan to remove one or two shrubs completely after three or four years.

• The wooden storage chests, illustrated in the plan view, should be treated to an annual coat of paint.

E LEVATED
GARDENS

A true roof garden is a desirable asset. Problems of access, water supply, safety considerations, and gusts of wind should be regarded as mild challenges that pale into insignificance when set against the potential rewards. Even tiny corners between chimney pots can be turned into miniature roof gardens, and you could use the space outside a mansard window to place planters or boxes on bricks, raising them high enough to let water run freely, and making their flowering contents visible from within.

If you have a flat roof offering good access, reasonable space, and distinct possibilities, do a little homework before you embark on turning it into a garden. Make sure the planning department of your local town has no objections, check that there is no fire-escape ladder already in position, requiring free access, inspect existing down-pipes and drainage to insure that they will accommodate the additional flow from plant watering and will not get blocked by soil and leaves, and,

ABOVE *This enticing roof top, secret and flowery, with its planting of soaring hollyhocks, roses and clematis, is a cottage garden in the sky.*

LEFT *These cleverly placed terracotta planters, against the perimeter wall, make the most of a limited space while year-round interest is provided by evergreen planting.*

finally, look at the roof's present covering. It is wise to consult an engineer, an architect, or a surveyor before embarking on anything structural.

Weight must always be considered when planning an elevated garden, and you should involve a professional when calculating the weight-bearing properties of your roof, if your ideas are ambitious. Generally speaking, the perimeter walls of any flat roof will be load-bearing, and you can set window boxes or planters on these, provided they are securely attached. In older houses, the joists forming the roof may not be strong enough to support a roof garden, in which case they should be strengthened first.

The next step is to erect some form of boundary, such as railings or a fence, to surround the space. Ideally, you would add some form of trellis or hurdle on top to provide a baffle for the winds that swirl about city roofs; winds are always unpredictable, but trellis lets them filter more temperately. A

combination of unbreakable solid glass and metal screening, as provided in some modern apartment blocks, offers both privacy and shelter. Should it be impossible to attach any form of rail or screen, you could consider planting a hedge of wind-resistant shrubs and trees in deep planters as a shelter-belt for other plants on your roof. The most wind- and drought-resistant evergreen barriers are *Thuja plicata* 'Atrovirens' (Z 5-7), *Pinus nigra* (Z 4-7) and sea buckthorn (*Hippophae rhamnoides,* Z 3-8).

The ideal way to combine shelter and containers in one operation would be to build a trellis structure that incorporated decorative planters at its feet, perhaps in the form of a wooden trough into which you could fit a plastic liner. To build the trellis, use battens no finer than ¾in x 1¼in and apply a coat of suitable outdoor protective paint or varnish. Such a structure would be both stable and practical; it could even incorporate a lidded bench-seat for storage as well as somewhere to sit.

Roofs may be one-sided, such as those above an extension, when the house or apartment itself provides shelter on one side, thus making the wind less trouble-some. Heating from below renders these gardens more or less frost-free, and if you install attractive artificial grass combined with ornamental trellis, an airy

LEFT *This appealing garden is composed of several levels of climber-clad, decorative trellis which, painted white, bring a sense of space to a tiny roof.*

extra room lies before you, awaiting decoration with plants. Where there is more space, an awning fixed to the house wall, and decorative pillars, used for twining climbers, creates a soft entrance to an outdoor room. Planting, matching the decorative scheme inside, can be spread all around the perimeter, or restricted to a pair of formal boxes.

If you have a created an outdoor room, it can be made still more enchanting through the installation of lighting. This can add magic to elevated gardens, making it a joy to sit outside sipping a soothing drink, or a pleasure to watch the shadows and shapes of plants from within if your space is too small to sit out. Again, the installation of an outdoor lighting circuit is best done by a qualified electrician well before you get involved in the planting. A more portable option is provided by freestanding storm lanterns and barbecue candles.

THE SURFACE

A soft asphalt roof will require some form of covering, such as plain light-weight tiles, to withstand the wear and tear of people. Where the roof is strong enough, terracotta-colored French Provençal-style tiles are both easy to clean and make a perfect background for decorative pots. Wooden decking is both pleasing and practical, spreading the weight of planters and protecting the roof below. This can be constructed out of hardwood or softwood that has been pressure-treated with a preservative, and laid on a hardwood sub-frame. The hazard of wooden decking is that debris will fall through the wooden battens and build up gradually, or, if there is a skylight, darken the room below. The best solution is to make the decking in removable sections, to allow for lifting and cleaning. If there is a raised skylight, which cannot be masked, decking brings the surface up to the same level.

Artificial grass is widely available today, and can be laid in a sheet; if the roof is exposed to winds, it can be attached firmly to the surface using a special adhesive. This artificial turf will stop debris falling through, although it is permeable, and it can be hosed down from time to time;

BELOW *The striking harlequin water feature and pots of pelargoniums have transformed this small garage roof into an elegant garden.*

it with your prettier, flower-filled arrangements. A striking effect would be created with a *Eucalyptus gunnii* (Z 7-10), kept pollarded, an *Elaeagnus* x *ebbingei* 'Gilt Edge' (Z 6-9) or an *Ilex aquifolium* 'Golden King' (Z 6-9), used singly or as a group of three. Changes can be rung throughout the year, leaving the tree in position while seasonal plantings of spring bulbs or summer bedding change at its feet. This system can be used for climbers too, whose roots also require spreading-space.

BALCONIES

Balconies are certainly elevated, though many appear to be sadly ignored, only one or two in some apartment blocks showing a fringe or frill of green. But you may see others, with ropes of ivy, billows of pelargoniums, and rivers of lobelia, which lift your spirits and make you forget all about city gloom. One well-filled planter is enough for a start, or a single tree in an old oil can, with perhaps a few herbs to provide living greenery.

Heavy window boxes set on top of concrete walls may appear secure, but it is wise to attach them firmly, either with a strong bolt driven through the drainage holes in the base into the wall coping, or held with brackets screwed to the wall. Severe gales can lift even heavy objects, and tall trees and shrubs merely act as a sail, so it is important to make everything secure before attempting to plant.

As in all small spaces, be selective with

provided attention has been paid to drainage, the water should drain away.

PLANTS AND WATERING

Watering is a vital consideration in all elevated gardens since most of the planting is in pots and boxes, which dry out especially fast when contending with wind and sun. Carrying cans of water out to the roof soon becomes a chore, so always remember to fit an outside tap on your roof. You might even consider installing one of the excellent self-watering systems now available; these are either computer-controlled or linked to a moisture-sensor in the soil. If you do this,

ABOVE *The mixture of rounded hosta leaves, delicate bamboo, spiky cordyline, hydrangea, box and hebe filling this minuscule spot leaves just enough space for table and chairs.*

arrange for a separate outlet or faucet for hand watering as well, so that you can give extra cosseting to a particular plant, or even wash down the roof from time to time.

Large shrubs or trees will require a container at least 20in in diameter to grow in, preferably more. The best solution might be to form a group comprised of one large container, flanked by two or three smaller, more decorative ones, enabling you to use something simple but spacious and mask your colors and plant combinations, choosing those that blend with the room inside. Remember that all the plants will tend to face away from you, and try to climb outward and downward. Colors that are too delicate and muted may also fail to stand out against concrete, so opt for brighter colors than you would normally choose for your garden.

A second planter or line of planters can be fixed on brackets lower down the concrete walls, on the side facing you. This would create a solid wall of plants, making a delightful view from your window and yet reserving the balcony area for chairs or tables. This lower level will always be in shade, so you could plant the classic dwarf conifers, pelargoniums, lobelias, and trailing verbenas on the top layer, with small euonymus, trailing ivies and patience plants below, all mingling within a few weeks until no bare concrete can be seen. If you have an ugly view of the next building, a large *Cordyline australis* (Z 10) in the middle of the top layer would help to screen it, while the waving spikes add movement to the scene. Despite being classed as a house or greenhouse plant in winter in the North, it and many seaside standbys, such as elaeagnus, brooms, escallonias and fuchsias stand up quite well before winter arrives in earnest in the North. A more interesting arrangement for a balcony, or a roof garden, would be to combine the planters with urns. This would be particularly effective if your perimeter walls were uniformly square or rectan-

gular. Position the urns on the corners, or use wooden planters, ending with large, square boxes planted with trees or climbers, to create a living buttress of plants.

ABOVE *Surrounded by spreading trees and billowing climbers, this roof garden, with its well-kept wooden decking, has the air of a simple Japanese-style garden.*

A TINY ROOF GARDEN

The soft colors, scents and textures of this sunny roof garden have a distinctly Mediterranean feel. It has the added bonus of a back wall and thus infinite possibilities for embellishment. The false doorway, attached to the blank wall, gives the garden another dimension, while the antique, teak door, surrounded by a matching frame, looks simple and rustic. The ornamental trellis on both sides, painted a soft blue-green, provides privacy and shelter, and the terracotta color of the Provençal tiles is echoed by the surrounding planters.

If you have a less sunny aspect, you could paint the trellis white for extra light, and replace the terracotta planters with crisp white wood and glazed pots.

ATTACHING THE FALSE DOOR

Screw the door directly onto the wall, using long screws and plugs, four in each corner. Insure that the door is set about 4in above the finished floor level to leave room for the stone step below the door. Screw and plug the door frame to the wall; the door frame is made of rough sawn lumber and stained silver-gray to match the faded door.

A MEDITERRANEAN WINDOW

Instead of a false door, attach a window, complete with a frame, shutters and a windowbox filled with cheerful gera-

RIGHT *This false window, with its striking green shutters and prettily planted window box, looks out onto a simple Mediterranean scene, which has been painted directly on the house wall of this roof garden.*

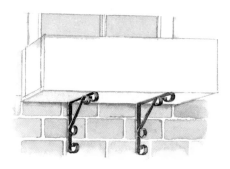

niums. Attach a discarded window frame to the wall, or make the window, complete with two cross bars to form four "panes," from a simple wooden rectangle.

MAINTENANCE

• Install an outside faucet for watering.
• Water the plants regularly, especially if exposed to the drying winds and sunshine that can afflict roof gardens.

PLANT LIST

From left to right:
• A trough of mostly tender bedding plants: *Solanum jasminoides* 'Album,' *Pelargonium* 'L' Elégant,' soft blue and mauve petunias, *Heliotropium* 'Princess Marina'
• A trough of *Melianthus major* and *Scaevola aemula* 'Blue Wonder' with thyme
• A pot containing a standard *Rosa* 'The Fairy' underplanted with parsley
• A trough of *Pittosporum tobira* (Z 9-10), *Argyranthemum frutescens*, *Felicia amelloides* 'Santa Anita' and *Verbena* 'Silver Anne'
• A pair of standard *Cupressus glabra* (Z 7-9) underplanted with *Viola cornuta* 'Belmont Blue'
• A pot of *Citrus x sinensis* 'Meyer'(Z 10)
• A trough of *Trachelospermum jasminoides* (Z 8-10)
• A pot of *Lilium regale*

MAINTAINING
TINY GARDENS

According to Dr Johnson, "What is written without pain is seldom read with pleasure," and we can apply this analogy to a garden: quite simply one created without a struggle will never enchant. It is important to realize that not only do truly tiny gardens need exceptional maintenance, but that you must be prepared to remove and replace the plants much more frequently than in the larger garden. Plants under stress because they are crammed into a small space, jostled by neighbors, deprived of light, or buffeted by fierce winds and scorched by blistering sun, are unlikely to survive indefinitely. They may also have to endure frequent pruning to provide space and let light in, and they may be plagued incessantly by aphids and other ailments. However tenderly we feed, water and spray them, many will eventually succumb or dwindle away sadly, and out they must go.

All this may sound daunting, implying that you will be continually trotting around your tiny garden, spraying, cutting back, and digging up. This is entirely wrong: your aim should be to do very little of any chore, but to do it regularly, in order to prevent your ever having to do a vast amount. Just as you might flick a duster over your furniture when you have a spare moment, so try and tweak off a dead-head or two as you pass, and have a quick spray while waiting for a meal or a particular television program. If you enjoy pottering, and regard the daily dead-heading, pest inspection, and blossom count as a good antidote to a stressful life, there is always scope to do more, but if your time is strictly limited, you should let "little and often" be your gardening motto.

GARDEN HYGIENE

Cleaning and tidying a tiny space is vital: nothing looks uglier than moribund plants, heaps of rubbish, or piles of discarded plastic pots. Keep within easy reach a brush (long- and short-handled if space permits) and a dustpan, along with a supply of plastic bags, and always aim to clear up after doing any gardening.

Ideally, a cupboard or box in the garden itself should have room for brushes, dustpan, bags, pruners, hand fork and trowel, one spray bottle for foliar feeding, another for the insecticides, the fertilizer and the pest controls you use, rolls of wire, vine eyes or wall nails, and any specific requirements such as fish food or slug pellets. If there is no space in the garden, make sure equipment is kept indoors within arm's length.

FEEDING AND WATERING

Plants which are confined and restricted, and thus forced to live somewhat unnatural lives, must be given compensation in the form of better feeding and watering than they would encounter in the wild, especially during their main growth period. A weak solution of any balanced general-purpose organic fertilizer, tomato fertilizer, or liquid manure should be added weekly to all containers filled with bedding plants, or window boxes that are crammed to overflowing. Tuck in slow-release nutrient tablets and feeding sticks

after planting, following the manu-facturer's instructions, and add water-retaining granules to hanging baskets and awkward-to-reach pots. Shrubs, trees and climbers require feeding less often, but I still feed them once a month during spring and early summer. Roses are best treated with the food especially formu-lated for them. They should be given one dose in early spring, and another after their first flush of flowers, then mulched with organic material in late autumn.

Watering should take priority over all else when the garden is in pots, in a shady passageway or basement, high up on a roof and exposed to drying winds, or surrounded by walls and paving. The lush growth you admire in well-cared-for plots owes more to regular and careful watering than to feeding. Learn to feel with your fingers whether soil is dry below the surface, and to water slowly

ABOVE *The well-swept paving, retaining walls and neatly clipped hedges, in this tiny back garden, create an air of crisp elegance.*

and thoroughly. Water should trickle from the bottom of a container before you stop, and one good periodic soak is better than daily splashes on your beds. In summer, aim to water three times a week, if you cannot manage it daily; in winter, check any pots regularly, and water only when they are really dry, and never in frosty weather.

PEST. AND DISEASE CONTROL

Most insecticide labels advise adding a measured amount of water to dilute the very concentrated solution in the bottle. Always do your measuring properly, and insure you are mixing your smaller amounts in the correct quantities. A spray holding 2 pints is a useful size for insecticides and mildew treatments, but it is wise to keep one dispenser for these alone, and a separate one for diluted liquid feed. This size is convenient for a garden with a number of plants, but should your garden only have a few plants, the ready-mixed spray cans might prove easier.

Before treating any plant immediately with selective measures, try removing aphids and other pests by hand, pulling them away between the fingers. Caterpillars are easily spotted and whisked off, as are snails and slugs, but whiteflies on fuchias require treatment. Leaf-cutting bees, fond of rose leaves for nest building, can be swotted with a rolled-up newspaper. The woodlice that you find scuttling about whenever you lift a pot are fairly harmless, feeding mainly on decaying leaves, so tidiness will deter them. Hunt for snails and slugs in the evening, and remove them; the proprietary pellets are best put down little and often. If removing the pests by hand does not work, plants can also be hosed down with plain water, or splashed with soapy water.

If you have lilies, the lily beetle, bright red and easily visible, should be removed instantly, before it goes on to lay its black, slimy eggs on the undersides of the foliage. Growers advise dowsing the growing medium, while the lily bulbs are dormant, with a powerful disinfectant,

ABOVE *This cleverly disguised compost can become part of the decorative scheme in a limited space, by supporting pots of colorful pelargoniums and rooted cuttings.*

RIGHT *This neat storage box for tools also makes an effective bench in the garden.*

diluted with water in 1:40 proportions, to prevent the problem before it arises.

Thus, your basic disease-prevention kit should include: slug and snail remedies; a selective aphid spray that leaves most beneficial insects unharmed; and a fungicide for mildew. You may also need a special rose compound, which combines prevention and cure for aphids and black spot, and a specific spray to tackle bay or box sucker. A degree of ruthlessness is often necessary if a plant is obviously ailing, with mildew, fungus mites, thrips or leaf miners. Consult your Cooperative Extension Service for regional advice, including repellants.

PLANTING AND PROPAGATING

Besides the general maintenance of our small spaces, we have to consider planting, seed-sowing, the taking of cuttings, removals and replacements. Few limited areas will allow for more than the dropping of a few seeds, such as nasturtiums, sunflowers (*Helianthus*), ipomoeas, sweet peas, *Cobaea scandens*, poppies (*Papaver*) or nigellas, into pots. A small gap in a crowded flowerbed may just permit you to tuck in a few of the tiny plants that you have started elsewhere, while a corner can usually be made for a tray of peat and sand in equal proportions, or vermiculite, ready to take cuttings of any desirable plant.

If you are able to overwinter young stock of marguerites, felicias, penstemons, argyranthemums and osteospermums, you will save yourself a fortune. They are easy to root in late summer, and can be grown on and protected in winter before being planted in their flowering positions in spring, when all danger of frost is past. Small, doll's house-sized greenhouses, heated by an electric light bulb, would give enough protection, and many a window sill inside can be used to start seeds in early spring. Even better is reliable sunshine indoors from a table top fluorescent light (or a reasonable shoplight fixture) kept on for 16 hours per day.

PRUNING

As the year progresses you will find your shrubs becoming blowsier and developing smothering tendencies, each trying to reach more light, so constant tieing back to fence or trellis is important, combined with judicious pruning. Sticking bamboo sticks into the earth through forward-leaning shrubs is a good way of forcing them back, or you could push them in at the back of your bed and attach them to the plant with wire. Turning pots or boxes from time to time prevents their developing bare patches and a regular half-turn is better than an annual volte-face.

Never be afraid to cut back whenever a shrub or tree spreads too far out of its allotted space: first look at its overall shape, and always cut back to a joint rather than in mid-branch. Extremely rampant climbers or wall shrubs such as *Solanum crispum* 'Glasnevin,' and *Solanum*

jasminoides (Z 9-10), *Actinidia kolomikta* (Z 4-9), many clematis and honeysuckles may be cut right back to the thick, trunk-like wood, both in early spring and at intervals during the summer.

Some evergreen shrubs can also be cut back severely in order to keep them within our tiny confines. These include *Arbutus unedo*, *Choisya ternata*, *Rhamnus alaternus*, *Daphne odora* (all Z 7-9), *Mahonia japonica* (Z 6-8), *Sarcococca humilis* (Z 5-8) as well as pittosporums, osmanthus, and camellias. Trees such as *Acer negundo* 'Flamingo' (Z 3-7) and *Eucalyptus gunnii* (Z 7-10) may be pollarded (their branches cut back to the trunk) annually or biannually if necessary, and conifers such as *Chamaecyparis lawsoniana* (Z 5-8) may be formed into standards by trimming their branches down to the trunk and shortening the tops.

P LANT DIRECTORY

Key to symbols

Zones

1	below –50°F
2	–50°F to –40°F
3	–40°F to –30°F
4	–30°F to –20°F
5	–20°F to –10°F
6	–10°F to 0°F
7	0°F to 10°F
8	10°F to 20°F
9	20°F to 30°F
10	30°F to 40°F

Aspect

◯ Sun

◑ Light shade

● Shade

● The size of the plants in the *Trees and shrubs*, *Climbers* and *Grasses and bamboos* sections is denoted by the following categories:

Small: not exceeding 2ft
Medium: not exceeding 8ft
Large: up to 20ft

TREES AND SHRUBS

In time, almost all trees and shrubs will outgrow a tiny space, however assiduously you prune and restrict them. For this reason, ultimate height and width measurements become somewhat academic with regard to very small gardens. It is also important to remember that any plant grown in a container or a raised bed, whose roots are necessarily restricted, will be slower to reach its full height than one in the ground. Bear in mind also that low light levels generally cause plants to become leggy and etiolated.

Trees

Acer negundo 'Flamingo' Box elder
Large ◯/◑ Zone 3-7
This native of North America is elegant and decorative, producing striking variegated leaves in shades of cream, pink and soft green. It responds cheerfully to drastic cutting back.

Amelanchier x *grandiflora* 'Forest Prince'
Large ◯/◑ Zone 5-8
A really tiny space might be overwhelmed by this beautiful shadbush, but though bushy and spreading in form, it is slow growing and fulfills our criterion of being multi-talented. The white flowers appear in spring along the bare stems, followed by leathery dark green leaves handsome all summer. In autumn, foliage flames to orange and red. This tree dislikes limy soil and prefers moist acid soil with good drainage.

Betula pendula 'Purpurea' European birch
Medium ◯/● Zone 3-6
This purple-leaved form is graceful and ornamental. As an exceptionally slow-growing plant, barely changing in ten years, it is wonderful for small spaces. I grow it in a north-facing bed, where its deep purple leaves dangle over a group of hellebores.

Caragana arborescens 'Pendula'
Medium ◯/◑/● Zone 2-8
These small shrubby trees from Siberia and Manchuria are tough enough to withstand gale-force winds and icy temperatures, making them ideal candidates for roof gardens. Their fretted, fern-like leaves emerge bright, fresh green in spring, and are followed by yellow pea flowers. This cultivar also has a pretty, weeping form and requires little in the way of attention.

Ligustrum lucidum 'Glossy privet'
Medium ☼/◐ Zone 7-10
Among the evergreen privet family, often unfairly overlooked due to its dullness and strong fragrance, are many excellent performers for small spaces. One form has brightly variegated leaves, mottled deep yellow and creamy white, and grows into a small tree with charm and character. Another cultivar, *L. lucidum* 'Tricolor,' has narrow, gray-green leaves, tinged pink when young, and forms a graceful, arching small tree.

Pittosporum tobira 'Variegata'
Large ☼ Zone 8-10
This pretty, evergreen native of New Zealand forms a dense column, thick and bushy. Its grayish-green leaves are edged with cream, and it produces orange blossom scented flowers in spring or early summer. During a cold spell in winter, its leaves take on a pinkish, mottled hue, and after a spring pruning, the new growth is deliciously fresh, its creamy edges like lacy frills. It will stand quite severe cutting back.

Shrubs

Large shrubs take on the role of trees in a very small garden, and also perform as climbers when placed against walls. Evergreen shrubs form the bones of any year-round scheme, and those with decorative or variegated foliage add lightness and elegance to sunken gardens and courtyards.

Artemisia tridentata Big sagebrush
Large ☼ Zone 4-9
A native of western N. America with aromatic silvery filigreed leaves, perhaps more evocative of cowboys and deserts than cottage and country gardens, although it

should fit in them, too. It tolerates container life as well as being planted in a raised bed or small planting space, where it grows into a tallish branching shrub. It makes a good foil for any color, and could support at least two climbers, forming a particularly good backdrop for roses.

It should be cut back in late spring to maintain its shape; if pot-grown, lift, divide and repot every three years. Shortening the growth regularly will keep it manageable.

Buddleia alternifolia Fountain buddleia
Medium ☼ Zone 5-10
This large shrub or small tree has delicately arching branches of narrow, dark green leaves, which are gray underneath and wreathed with deliciously scented, lilac flowers in midsummer. It is easily trained to form a small standard. When grown in a pot, it remains youthful for longer, and can support a frail clematis, such as *Clematis florida* 'Sieboldii.' It is important to shorten the long branches when necessary; and always to provide a stake for the trunk when freestanding.

Buxus sempervirens 'Variegata'
Small ☼/◐ Zone 5-9
A silver form of the well-known box, this shrub has small, rather irregular leaves with creamy white margins. It grows into a dense, compact shape, and can be used to make a low silvery hedge, or trained into any form and used as a focal point. When shaped, it blends with both silver and gold foliage, making it useful to dot around in groupings. It is happy to remain container-bound indefinitely.

Camellia
Medium/Large ◐ Zone 7-9
No book covering tiny, awkwardly placed gardens could ignore this wonderful genus of

evergreen shrubs, with their delectable flowers, which will grow and flower even in deep shade. Their flowers may be single, semi-double, anemone-centered, peony-centered or formal double, in shades of all reds through to pure white. For our purposes we must restrict ourselves to slow-growing or compact forms: 'Coral Delight' (*C. japonica* and *C. saluensiscross*), semi-double coral pink flowers, slow-growing; 'Freedom Bell' (*C. japonica* and *C. saluensiscross*), rather small semi-double red flowers; 'Professor C. R. Sargent' (*C. japonica*), dark red double flowers, compact bush; 'Nuccio's Pearl' (*C. japonica*), double orchid-pink flowers, compact bush; 'Bert Jones' (*C. sasanqua*), semi-double pink flowers with yellow stamens, slow-spreading plant. Camellias thrive in near neutral or acid soil, with added peat; ideal for containers.

Caryopteris x clandonensis 'Heavenly Blue'
Small ☼ Zone 5-9
This bushy shrub is grown for its aromatic, silvery leaves and deep blue flowers freely produced in late summer when their delicacy contrasts well with midsummer's tendency to become overblown and heavy. They like a slightly neutral soil, and are unsuitable for dank corners, but would give a welcome fillip to a sunny roof.

Ceanothus California-lilac
Medium ☼ Zone 7, 8-9
The rich blue flowers and neat, shiny evergreen leaves make this shrub valuable for warm, sheltered sites such as the West Coast and parts of Pacific NW. As a genus, they are short-lived but fast-growing, so eminently suited to our small spaces, provided good drainage can be given. Less vigorous climbers can be effectively woven through them. *C.*

'Concha' and C. 'Frosty Blue' may flower twice and remain fairly small. C. *thyrsiflorus repens* forms a wide, low mound smothered in bright blue flowers, and is good for growing over a wall. Any shortening required is best carried out directly after flowering.

Ceratostigma willmottianum
Small ◐ Zone 5-8

Sometimes thought of as being a hardy perennial, this sub–shrub produces rich, clear blue flowers from late summer to late autumn, when the small, rounded leaves turn all shades of red. It is an undemanding candidate for a sunny corner, content to be ignored, cut back or even smothered by other plants, and remaining well below its maximum height of 3ft.

Clethra alnifolia 'Hummingbird' Summersweet
Medium ◐/◑ Zone 3-9

Almost made to order for smaller gardens is this new form of native summersweet. 'Hummingbird' has all the good qualities of the species – spicy, summery scent from creamy flower spikes above rough, woodsy foliage – but on a much shorter shrub (about 3 ft). Use as ground cover, backing for ferns and hostas in part shade or as accents near terrace. It likes humusy, moist soil.

Cotoneaster
Small/Medium ◐/◑/● Zone 4-9

C. *dammeri* (Z 5-9) is a useful, decorative shrub for crawling along an awkward corner or wall. Although generally regarded as "ground cover," it would slot nicely into passageways and throughways, being evergreen and producing scarlet berries in autumn. C. 'Coral Beauty' has a tendency to mound rather than creep. C. *salicifolius* (Z 6-9) and C. *apiculatus* (Z 4-9) make a charming, small weeping tree when grown on a

stem, useful as an upright shape whose trailing, glossy, evergreen branches carry masses of brilliant red fruits in autumn and winter. C. *horizontalis* (Z 4-9) makes its engaging fishbone-outline as it climbs upwards against a wall, producing berries and coloring to a rich red in autumn, smothered in bees in summer and flourishing even in cold, shaded positions. Although deciduous, it forms a good background in a raised bed or awkward corner, and is easily cut back if necessary. 'Variegatus' is a pretty, white-edged version, less vigorous and shy of berrying, but producing a soft, grayish effect when seen from a distance, with a long-lasting deep pink coloring in the autumn.

Euonymus fortunei
Small ◐/◑/● Zone 5-9

These cheerful plants are invaluable in small and shady gardens, and their creamy-white variegations brighten the most unpromising corners. They remain low and creeping, or will hoist themselves up a wall and become self-clinging. 'Emerald Gaiety' has rounded leaves; those of 'Silver Queen' are more pointed; both have pale yellow young growth in spring. 'Emerald 'n' Gold' is brighter still.

Fothergilla gardenii Dwarf fothergilla
Medium ◐/◑ Zone 5-8

Another native dwarf shrub (3ft) for the informal small-space garden. Its white bottle-brush flowers, lightly fragrant, appear in spring as leaves open. 'Blue Mist' has blue-green foliage. Autumn leaf color of it and species is in bright reds and yellows. Grow in sun or light shade and moist but well-drained soil.

Hebe
Small/Medium ◐ Zone 8-10

A splendid group of species, mainly from

New Zealand and now very much at home in much of the West Coast. They offer good foliage and pleasing shapes. H. *pinquifolia* is silvery with purple-blue flowers. H *rakaiensis*, one of my favorites, has warm clear green leaves, and forms a neat hedge. H. *topiaria*, small and neat, with gray-green leaves, is a perfect accent in a decorative urn – it is really a minuscule topiary for the minuscule space.

Rosa Rose
Small/Medium/Large ◐ Zone 2-9

In tiny spaces, provided there is sun, roses will provide flowers over a long period, and most people will want to include at least one. 'Aloha' (Z 5-9) is my favorite to grow as a climber, although it is actually more of a large shrub. It is healthy and handsome, an important consideration in a genus riddled with ailments, and its deep terracotta-pink, scented flowers seem to carry on all summer. 'Graham Thomas,' (Z 5-9) a warm-yellow tea rose, becomes a tall shrub in a larger garden, but in a limited space makes a substitute for a climber, grown against a back wall. 'Mary Rose'(Z 5-9) produces sweetly scented, old-fashioned blooms over a long time, and, though slow to get started, it is splendid once established. 'Nathalie Nypels' (Z 5-9) is an excellent choice for a miniature sunny garden; it has soft-pink cluster roses, with a hint of yellow at the base, flowering almost continuously during summer, with dark, glossy leaves. 'Margaret Merril' (Z 5-9) is a ravishing, sweetly scented rose whose double white flowers have palest pink hints. 'Fair Bianco' (Z 5-9), sold as a patio rose (therefore dwarf), will grow to a height of 3ft; it throws up pretty, little button sprays, creamy and prolific, all summer. 'The Fairy' (Z 3-9) and 'Ballerina' (Z 6-10) make charming standards. For the tiniest of spaces, the miniature roses, in full bud, as sold in florists and garden centers from early summer, could be bought as a treat; choose your color with care and make it a focal point in your bedding scheme, giving it away or discarding it at the end of a season.

CLIMBERS

Climbers add the precious third dimension we need, enabling us to use walls, railings, and fences as an extension to our limited space. Among this group I include wall plants as well as true climbers for the role they play in our tiny gardens.

Clematis
Medium/Large ◐/◑ Zone 3-9

Though most clematis species and cultivars are too vigorous for our small spaces, there are several forms that are irresistible, at least in the short term, both for their ability to clamber up a shrub and for their own decorative qualities. *C. alpina* (Z 3-9) bursts into growth in early spring, threading its light, fresh green leaves through a host shrub before producing its pretty, nodding flowers: 'Willy,' mauve-pink flowers; 'Pamela Jackman,' deep purple bells; 'Helsingborg,' blue-purple flowers. *C. alpina* and its hybrids are rugged; if vines are cut back after flowering, a second crop may appear in summer. *C. macropetala* (Z 5-9) is a similar species with a double flower form: 'Markham's Pink' is a marvelous old rose shade. *C. chrysocoma* (syn. *spooneri*) (Z 5-9), known as the dogwood clematis, has a blanket of white flowers with creamy stamens. All these need watching, as they can overwhelm their site unless you are firm with the pruners.

C. viticella (Z 5-9) is a later flowering group, and should be cut down to base in early spring. It is perfect for training up a spring-flowering shrub; if it becomes too vigorous, it may need a second shortening. All varieties flower in summer on the new wood: 'Polish Spirit' (Z 4-9) is a glorious deep violet; 'Royal Velours,' an intense wine-purple; 'Purpurea Plena Elegans' (Z 4-9), a double soft reddish-purple and 'Mme. Julia Correvon' (Z 3-9), rosy-red blooms with golden stamens. The slightly less hardy evergreen *C. armandii* (Z 7-9) has dark, shining pointed leaves: 'Snowdrift' produces a mass of pure white, scented blossoms in spring. Again, cut right back to a low pair of new growths immediately after flowering, as the coppery new leaves sprout just as the flowers fade.

Clianthus puniceus Red parrot-beak
Medium ◯ Zone 8-9

This rare tender evergreen is a wall shrub, with elegant pinnate leaves and astonishing "lobster claw" flowers appearing in summer. There is a good white form, 'Albus' and various forms from New Zealand in deep rosy-pink, scarlet and white, tinged with green. Choose a very sheltered sunny wall for this plant, and provide trellis for it to spread over; a sunny position in a sunken garden or even a throughway might prove ideal, and the reward would be a spectacular and impressive sight. It needs to be kept fairly dry during winter but allowed plenty of moisture, both at its roots and around the foliage, during summer.

Fremontodendron californicum Flannel bush
Large ◯ Zone 9-10

This tender, semi-evergreen shrub requires a sheltered wall to produce its large, solid yellow flowers all summer long, among the olive-green, hairy leaves. The whole plant is

so hairy as to be almost prickly, and so bright a yellow that it requires careful placing, but it gets good marks for great cheerfulness. Plant it as far away as your space allows, to shine brightly on a distant wall.

Hedera helix helix English ivy
Small ◯/◐/● Zone 5-9

No garden, small or vast, should be without ivies in some form, and their amazing versatility makes them champions of the tiny space. Use them as ground cover, climbers, topiary, edge softeners, trailers for hanging baskets and windowboxes, and a backcloth for flowering climbers. Study the bewildering varieties of shape, coloring and habit on offer in garden centers and from specialist nurseries; all thrive in any soil and any position, but the variegated leaves tend to revert to green in shade. Perhaps the most valuable for small spaces are: 'Silver dust,' small to medium-sized, rich green leaves with white margins; 'Little Diamond,' pointed silver leaves, bushy in form; 'Manda's Crested,' nicknamed 'Curly Locks' for the wavy-edged, medium-sized green leaves, turning to red in the autumn; 'Pixie,' white-veined small green leaves, with crinkled edges.

Jasminum polyanthum Jasmine
Large ◯ Zone 8-10

This species is less vigorous than the summer jasmine (*J. officinale*), which it otherwise resembles, but which is altogether too much for the tiny garden. Grown on a sheltered wall, its exquisitely scented white flowers will flood the air. *J.* x *stephanense* (Z 7-10) is a pretty hybrid whose leaves may be cream-variegated in early summer; its pale pink flowers blend well with pale blue felicias, pink diascias, or blue *Ceanothus* x *delileanus*.

Schizophragma hydrangeoides
Large   ◐/◑/●   Zone 5-8
This is a self-clinging relation of the hydrangea whose flowers resemble those of *Hydrangea petiolaris* and last for at least two months in midsummer. The young shoots take time to settle down and become properly attached to walls. Although it will eventually become too vigorous for the small garden, it will cover a blank, shaded wall, such as a passageway, with distinction in the meantime. 'Roseum' has clear pink flowers; 'Moonlight' has mottled, silvery-gray leaves.

Solanum jasminoides
Medium/Large   ◐/◑   Zone 9-10
This delightful tender twining climber, whose white flowers start in late spring and carry on undaunted until the first frosts, is one of the all-time stars for a sunny, sheltered garden. It rambles delightfully through shrubs, over trellis or up trees, but is content to be chopped back when it gets too enthusiastic. It may be cut back by infrequent cold spells, and is not a vine for the North but can be grown indoors.

Trachelospermum jasminoides Star jasmine
Small   ◐   Zone 8-10
A charming evergreen climber, requiring shelter but responding with a mass of deliciously scented, creamy flowers in midsummer; its shining leaves look polished. The gently twining plant deserves a protected corner where it could either be grown up an obelisk or a wigwam, or planted beside a seat or doorway, perhaps in a pretty pot in a front porch. Its variegated version seems shy to flower, but the gray-green leaves, which are edged with white, turn blush-pink in winter.

PERENNIALS

Few true perennials make ideal candidates for the tiny space. Many might appear suitable, and some survive for a few seasons, but experience has taught me that the list is short. However, those which are suitable can almost be classed as indispensable and they are listed.

Euphorbia Spurge
◐   Zone 3-9
The slightly tender *E. mellifera* (up to 4ft) is a favorite of mine, because of the brilliant, fresh apple-green of its foliage that lasts all year and is followed by strongly honey-scented flowers in early summer. *E. myrsinites* (Z 4-9) is a trailing edging plant requiring good drainage; excellent for the front of a raised bed or a retaining wall.

Helleborus Hellebore
◑/●   Zone 3-9
The evergreen *H. foetidus* (20in) (Z 5-8) is a good stand-by for shade and awkward corners, seeding itself with abandon. Groups planted in a dark corner will stretch out their dark green, fern-cut leaves, adding pale green, nodding flowers from late winter to late spring. *H. argutifolius* (2ft) (Z 5-9), also evergreen, with thick, spiny leaves and yellow-green flowers in spring, forms a handsome clump whose architectural shape makes a good foil for small daffodils.

Heuchera
◐/◑/●   Zone 3-9
This group of low-growing herbaceous evergreens (10-12in) provides valuable clumps of shapely leaves, with flowers over a long period throughout the summer. *H.* 'Coral Cloud' has dark green, handsome,

toothed leaves and pretty, drooping pink flowers. *H. cylindrica* (Z 4-8) has heart-shaped, clear green leaves, which mound up into a solid clump, from which it throws up long sprays of greenish-white flowers. *H. micrantha* 'Palace Purple' (Z 4-8) is deservedly popular, with its rich plum-colored leaves appearing in a variety of mixed plantings. It is a good edging plant for raised beds, at the feet of a small rose, or below clematis in a narrow passage. In full sun it becomes almost bronze but part-shade shows its lush, velvety coloring to perfection.

Heucherella tiarelloides
◑/●   Zone 4-8
This rosette-forming rounded perennial grows up to 6-9in. The evergreen leaves are frilled, and the tiny, bell-shaped pink flowers are produced in early summer. *H.* 'Bridget Bloom' throws up rosy-pink flowers at intervals from early summer until autumn, with its bright green leaves in a dense clump.

Liriope muscari
◐/◑/●   Zone 6-10
This evergreen spreading perennial (12in) throws thickly clustered spikes of purple-blue flowers, resembling grape hyacinths, clear of its narrow, strap-shaped, dark green leaves. Though not showy, it is a good plant for difficult and shady places, for example, as an edging below climbers in a passageway or bordering a low wall in deep shade.

Pulmonaria officinalis 'Sissinghurst White'
Common lungwort
◑/●   Zone 4-8
The long, pointed, white-spotted leaves of this lungwort (9-12in) are semi-evergreen and

its elegant, funnel-shaped white flowers are borne upright above the foliage for several weeks in spring. *P. longifolia* (Z 5-8) has longer, narrower leaves, also white-spotted, and brilliant blue flowers in late spring.

GRASSES AND BAMBOOS

The distinctive shape, foliage and line of these plants bring a valuable contrast to the form of most garden plants. The height and spread of both bamboos and grasses depend on the space you allow them; bear in mind that many will grow taller in shaded positions, but that they will remain well under control when grown in containers. Both grasses and bamboos make excellent roof garden plants, where they survive conditions of wind and exposure.

Arundinaria murieliae
Large   ☼/◐   Zone 7-9
Although this graceful arching bamboo grows to 10ft or more in an open spot, it is worth including here for its use as a windbreak or shelter in a small space. The bright pea-green leaves will remain decorative for most of the year while the canes, which start bright green, mature to a duller yellow-green color.

Carex oshimensis 'Evergold' Sedge
Small   ☼/◐/●   Zone 6-9
An invaluable evergreen grass, cheerful in even the most unpromising of positions where it presents its bright, stripy mop of yellow "hair" from any angle. It spreads slowly, occasionally adding small flower spikes in summer to its repertoire. It is a superb plant for filling an awkward corner, requiring minimal maintenance.

Hakonechloa macra 'Aureola'
Small   ☼   Zone 4-9
This is a splendidly showy, gold and green striped grass, ageing to reddish-brown. In a sunny spot, its waterfall of bright yellow is cheerful and bright. It is slow-growing and may produce panicles of reddish-brown flower spikes in early autumn, lasting into winter.

Helictotrichon sempervirens Blue oat grass
Medium   ☼   Zone 4-9
This elegant perennial grass produces silvery-blue leaves which are stiff and slender, with straw-colored flower spikes in summer. It can be grown in a pot or a well-drained bed.

Ophiopogon planiscapus 'Nigrescens'
Small   ☼/◐/●   Zone 6-9
This delectable small, black "grass," low and unshowy, offers rather dull pinkish flowers for only a short time; it is not to everyone's taste but is passionately admired by some. It creeps quietly along absolutely anywhere: in deep shade, under shrubs, between trees. Always smart and elegant, its glum clump evokes a smile whenever you spot it.

Pleioblastus variegatus
Medium   ☼/◐   Zone 7-10
The narrow leaves of this dwarf bamboo retain their clear white stripes all year round. It spreads slowly and, unlike other members of the tribe, branches near its base. Its habit is stiffer and less graceful than the more invasive species, but it is excellent for miniature gardens and is often used for an Oriental effect.

Pleioblastus viridistriatus
Small   ☼/◐/●   Zone 8-10
This engaging, yellow-striped small bamboo is not invasive; it spreads gently without smothering its neighbors, producing fresh stripy leaves in late spring that remain until winter. If it is cut right down in autumn, the new growth will emerge evenly, but if it is only shortened in early spring, you will have a taller, somewhat untidy clump. In shade, where it is perfectly happy, the color will be less brilliant; in sun it glows.

Trachycarpus fortunei Windmill palm
Medium   ☼/◐   Zone 8-10
This splendid, spiky palm, to be found towering over mild gardens, waving its huge sharp fronds over tender shrubs, will happily endure many years jammed into a pot on a well-protected roof where it will grow no taller than 2ft. It provides shape and style and can be the mainstay of an elegant design, throwing out a new frond or two regularly and remaining small and wide, rather than rearing upwards.

BEDDING PLANTS

These are the ephemeral, usually annual, colorful additions to the bones of our small gardens, which we count on to brighten up the spring and summer scene. More than with any other aspect of gardening, their selection depends entirely on your personal taste, combined with the aspect in which you use them. I concentrate here on the few which have proved themselves to me time and time again.

Brachyscome iberidifolia Swan river daisy
☼   Annual
These small, daisy-flowered annuals (6-9in) have finely cut bright green leaves, with a mass of tiny, bright blue, yellow-centered daisies that carry on throughout the summer.

Cordyline Palm–lily

☼ Zone 9-10

The ultimate size of these tropical elegant palm-like plants would be way beyond the limitations of our small spaces, but used as tender bedding plants or short-lived shrubs, and growing to 2-5ft, they are invaluable. They form centerpieces for windowboxes, or offer foliage contrast in a bed full of softer, rounded-leaved plants. As soon as they become too large or solid, which may happen in one season, donate them to a friend and start again with a young plant. In warm climates, the plant can be left to grow and form its true, spike-on-a-stem shape, perhaps in a pot of its own, and moved about as a handsome focal point. Two species, *C. australis* and *C. terminalis*, have several cultivars, usually sold in florist shops.

Erysimum Siberian wallflower

☼ Zone 3-9

This biennial, often perennial wallflower (16in) prefers poor soil, provided it is well-drained. It is especially useful for containers on a roof, or the front of a raised bed. Seeds sown early may flower first year. *E. allioni* 'Orange Bedder' has fragrant flowers.

Fuchsia Ladies eardrops

☼/◑/● Mostly Zone 9-10

The varied flowers in this enormous genus of deciduous or evergreen shrubs and trees carry on from early summer until mid-autumn. They possess an artificial air that renders them particularly suitable for small, cultivated spaces. *F. magellanica* 'Versicolor' (4ft) is moderately hardy (Z 7-9), its gray-green leaves edged with creamy-white and flushed with pink when young; the flowers are narrow, red and purple. Less showy than most, its soft foliage and shapely growth add style from late spring until late autumn, with the pretty dangling flowers a bonus in summer. *F.* 'Madame Cornelissen' (30in) is one of the oldest varieties, hardy, reliable, healthy and long-flowering, with upright, red-tinted foliage and semi-double flowers, white with bright scarlet. *F.* 'Tom Thumb' (20in) is a hardy, compact form, producing small flowers with red tubes and purple-mauve petals; upright-growing. *F.* 'Marinka' (10in), half-hardy and trailing, produces red flowers with darker, folded petals; this cultivar prefers a shaded, sheltered position.

Impatiens Patience plant

◑/● Annual

These familiar plants (12in) in all shades of red, pink and mauve, plain or striped, as well as white, are strictly evergreen bushy perennials, but they are grown as summer annuals because they are frost tender. Happy in any aspect, they will continue flowering from spring until the first frosts, if well-fed and watered.

Salvia farinacea 'Victoria'

☼ Zone 9-10

This bedding plant (18in) produces spikes of deep violet-blue flowers, with strong upright stems of the same ravishing color. In full sun in an open position, it will carry on until autumn, blending well with all colors.

Scaevola aemula 'Blue Wonder'

☼/◑

One of the most satisfactory summer bedding plants (2ft), this has deep green foliage and masses of rich, mauve-blue flowers that continue through the season, undaunted by rain or gloom. Its habit is to trail and form a rising mound, each layer of flowers and foliage seeming to climb above the next, creating a spreading mass of color and a giant hanging basket all on its own.

Verbena 'Peaches and Cream'

☼ Annual

This popular bedding plant is a 1993 AAS Award and Fleuroselect winner also suited to hanging baskets. It produces soft, sweetly scented peaches and cream flowers throughout the summer, spreading delicate ferny leaves from a container or weaving its way through other front-of-border plants.

BULBS

Provided you are prepared to treat them as short-term investments, many bulbs are invaluable for the tiny space. Some, such as tulips and lilies, look even better in containers than they do in a bed or border. Bulbs like hyacinths, narcissi (daffodils) and grape hyacinths (*Muscari*) that have been used in windowboxes or containers can always be lifted and removed to a larger garden, fed and watered, and left there to recover and continue to flower in future seasons. A few will carry on for a couple of years in captivity, but do not rely on it.

Crocus

☼ Zone 3-8

Spring-flowering, often scented, delicate and inspiring, these small corms (3-5in) can be tucked into a corner in the smallest space. *C. chrysanthus* 'Snow Bunting' is fragrant, with mustard-yellow centers to the white flowers; 'Cream Beauty,' also sweetly scented, is a buttery cream color with darker yellow inside and brownish-purple at the base. 'E.A. Bowles' is early-flowering, a clear, deep yellow and prettily scented; *C. vernus* 'Pickwick' is a soft pale lilac with darker stripes.

Hyacinthus Hyacinth
☼/◐ Zone 4-8

Treated as inhabitants of an outdoor "vase," hyacinths (6-10in), with their powerful, drenching sweetness, add enormously to the joys of spring. They can be bought already in flower at garden centers or florists and generally last far longer than you expect; they will return for two or three years when planted in small beds or sunny corners. The colors range from white through cream, yellows, blues, mauves to pink, so they can be mixed with spring bedding plants of all hues. Hyacinths need a well-drained soil.

Lilium Lily
☼ Zone 3-8

Few can fail to be enchanted by the ravishing beauty of these delectable bulbs, some of which add exquisite scent to their long list of charms. *L. regale* (20in-4ft) is the easiest of all to grow, with white trumpet flowers flushed with purple on the outside. Plant in well-crocked pots at least 12in in diameter in groups of three (or five when larger pots are available), in good garden soil enriched with organic matter; plant at least twice the depth of the bulb, covering the surface with leaf-mold if possible.

The Asiatic hybrids are a group containing many lilies with a dwarf habit. 'Apollo' (4ft) has fine, creamy white flowers, pinkish outside; 'Cote d'Azur' (4ft) is a lovely soft pink; 'Red Carpet' (12-18in) is short, with glowing, dark lipstick-red flowers.

The Oriental hybrids include some of the most deliciously scented lilies of all. 'Le Rêve' (28in) is a soft blue-pink with a sturdy stem; 'Star Gazer' (1-3ft) has broad crimson petals with maroon spots and a white border.

Muscari Grape hyacinth
☼ Zone 3-8

Pretty, upright stems of dense blue (or white) flowers on low plants in early spring (6-8in). Most will survive for two or three years in boxes and other containers.

Narcissus Daffodil
☼/◐ Zone 4,6,8

No spring garden would be complete without these entrancing trumpets nodding in howling winds. For the tiny space, the dwarf daffodils, known as *Narcissus cyclamineus*, *N. triandrus* and *N. tazetta* hybrids, are more successful, many of them being multi-headed and very long-lasting. 'Tête-à-tête' (6-12in) is widely available. 'Minnow' (7in) is delicate, pale yellow; 'Jumblie' (8in), pretty and engaging, and 'Jenny' (12in), a little taller, is a soft creamy white. 'Trena' and 'Tracey' (8in) are ravishing cultivars, in white and clear lemon yellow, and subtle white and cream respectively; most will grow reasonably in shade. 'February Gold' and 'February Silver' (13in), flowering a month later than their name implies, will usually last for several seasons.

Scilla siberica
☼/◐ Zone 2-3

Resembling a small English bluebell, these hardy little bulbs (4-6in) carry several stems of brilliant blue, bell-shaped flowers that last for several weeks. The strap-shaped leaves appear first, followed by flowers.

Tulipa Tulip
☼ Zone 3-8

Not even roses have as wide a color spectrum as these much-painted flowers. For growing in pots, the *kaufmanniana* and *greigii* types are considered most suitable, being less than 12in high and adding striped and mottled leaves to their charms. 'Red Riding Hood' (8in) lifts its lipstick-red flowers above beautifully marked leaves and is long-lasting; 'Imperial Splendour' (8in) has clear, primrose-yellow flowers and pretty foliage; 'Oratorio' (8in) is apricot-rose. All these are candidates for windowboxes or containers. *T. praestans* 'Fusilier' is an elegant tulip whose small, brilliant scarlet flowers are carried only 6in above the fresh, pale green leaves. Pointed petals add to its charms, and each stem bears several flowers, making it excellent value-for-space, well-suited to windowboxes and containers, which also provide the sharp drainage it prefers.

The taller varieties look better in good-sized pots or decorative planters. 'Apricot Beauty' (16in) has a mixture of rose and apricot colors and looks marvelous with old terracotta; 'Queen of Night' (25in) is almost black, lustrous and unusual; 'Shirley' (14in) opens to ivory-white, edged with soft mauve; 'Douglas Bader' (16in) is palest blush-pink with a deeper shade in the center of each petal and prettily rounded heads; 'White Triumphator' (26-28in), though tall, is strong, and carries its elegant flowers well above the foliage; 'Ballerina' (20-22in), a lily-flowered tulip in soft marigold, is also deliciously scented, a rarity among the breed.

Index

Note: Page numbers in *italic* indicate illustrations; numbers in **bold** to plants in the Plant Directory.

Acer
    A. japonicum 50
    A. negundo 20, 71, 85, **86**
    A. palmatum 15, *35*
Actinidia 32
    A. kolomikta 85
adornments 27–35
Agave 32
Ailanthus 32
Akebia quinata 10, 12
Alchemilla mollis 27, 32, 72
Amelanchier x *grandiflora* **86**
Ampelopsis 32
    A. glandulosa 33
Anemone 10
    A. x *hybrida* 57
aphids 13, 84
Aralia 32
    A. elata 60
Arbutus unedo 71, 85
arches 18, 66
Arctotis 19, 48
Argyranthemum *28*, 71
    A. frutescens 80
Artemisia 69
    A. tridentata **87**
Arundinaria 10
    A. murieliae **91**
Asplenium
    A. scolopendrium 53
    A. trichomanes 53
Athyrium
    A. filix-femina 53
    A. niponicum pictum 53
Aucuba 13, 50, *55*
    A. japonica 10, 57, 63
Azalea kiusianum 35

back gardens 65–73
balconies *65*, 78–9
bamboo 10, 32, 61, *78*, 91
battens 52
bay tree (*Laurus*) 22, *50*
bedding plants 91–2
Begonia 50, 55
Berberis 43
Bergenia 10, 43, 44, *45*, 51
Betula pendula 39, **86**
birch (*Betula*) 39, 67, 86
bonsai 30, *30*, 34, *35*
boulders 28–9, 31, 34
boundaries 18–19, *18*, 75–6
box (*Buxus*) 10, 19, 25, *33*, 43, 87
Brachyscome iberidifolia **91**
Buddleia alternifolia **87**
bulbs 92–4
Buxus 19, 25, *33*
    B. sempervirens 10, 43, **87**

Camellia 10, 25, 50, 61, 85, **87**
    C. japonica 63, 72
    C. x *williamsii* 63
Campanula 40, 48
Caragana arborescens **86**
Carex
    C. oshimensis *45*, 72, **91**
    C. pendula 32
Caryopteris x *clandonensis* **87**
Ceanothus 49, 67, 72, **87–8**
    C. thyrsiflorus repens 88
Ceratostigma 71
    C. willmottianum **88**
Cercis canadensis 60
Chaenomeles 10
Chamaecyparis
    C. lawsoniana 24, 85
    C. pisifera 35
chimney pots 51
Choisya ternata 41, 43, 48, 72, 85
Cimicifuga 10
Citrus x *sinensis* 80
Clematis 37, 41, 49, *59*, 85, **89**
    C. alpina 33
    C. armandii 50, 56

    C. macropetala 33
    C. maximowicziana 59
    C. montana rubens 56, 59
    C. viticella 22, 33, 47
Clethra alnifolia **88**
Clianthus puniceus **89**
climbers 10, 33, 50, 56, 71, 89–90
Clockvine (*Thunbergia*) 33
Cobaea scandens 33, *53*
Common Lugwort (*Pulmonaria*) **90–1**
containers 10–11, 29–30, 39, 56–7 *see also* adornments
Convallaria majalis 59
Cordyline 78, **92**
    C. australis 79, **92**
    C. terminalis **92**
Coronilla glauca 14, 15
Cosmos atrosanguineus 71
Cotoneaster **88**
    C. horizontalis 43
creeping jenny (*Lysimachia*) 55
Crocus **92–3**
Cupressus glabra 80
Cyclamen coum 45
Cyperus papyrus 32

daffodil (*Narcissus*) 93
Daphne
    D. laureola 10
    D. marginata 71
    D. odora 48, 71, 85
    D. pontica 59
dark gardens 9–15
decking 34, *41*, 48, *60*, 77, *79*
Diascia 71
Dicentra 10
disease control 84–5
doors 17, 18, 80
Dracaena cincta 24, 25

Elaeagnus 10, 19, 79
    E. x *ebbingei* 78
elevated gardens 75–80
entrances 37–45
Epimedium 10, 43

Erigeron 40
    E. karvinskianus *45*
Erysimum *45*, **92**
Escallonia 79
Eucalyptus 55
    E. gunnii 71, 78, 85
Euonymus 32, 43
    E. fortunei 10, 57, 63, 72, **88**
Euphorbia 32, **90**
    E. polychroma 35
European silver birch (*Betula*) 86

false boundaries 18–19, *18*
false doors 80
false floors 56, 62
false windows 48, 80, *80*
x *Fatshedera lizei* 63
Fatsia japonica 10, 13, *35*, 50, *55*, 63, 71
feeding 82–3
Felicia 19, 71
    F. amelloides 58–9, 80
ferns 10, 12, 50, 55, 58
Festuca ovina glauca 22, *45*, 72
floors, false 56, 62
flowering cherry (*Prunus*) 6
Fothergilla gardenii 88
fountains *23*, 32, *65*
Fremontodendron 72
    F. mexicanum **89**
front gardens 37–45
Fuchsia 29, *41*, 53, 63, 79, **92**

gardener's garters (*Phalaris*) 19
Gazania 19
Gleditsia triacanthos 60
golden hop (*Humulus*) 47
grape hyacinth (*Muscari*) *35*, 41, 93
grasses 77, 91
gravel 28–9, 47–8, *48*, 68, 69
Gunnera manicata 20

Hakonechloa macra 19, **91**
hanging baskets 56, 57
Hebe 32, 40, *78*, 79, **88**
    H. albicans 69

H. pinguifolia 45
H rakaiensis 25, 28
Hedera 13, 49, 56, 60
   H. helix helix 22, 25, 31, 63, 72,
   89
Helianthemum 48
Helichrysum petiolare 45
Helictotrichon sempervirens 32, **91**
Heliotropium 45, 80
Helleborus 10, 32, **90**
   H. foetidus 57
Heuchera **90**
   H. micrantha 45
Heucherella tiarelloides **90**
Hippophae rhamnoides 76
holly 10, 12, 13, 19, 42
honeysuckle 49, *59*, 60, *60*, 85
Hosta 10, 27, 30, 78
   H. fortunei 35
   H. sieboldiana 15
Humulus lupulus 47
Hyacinthus **93**
Hydrangea 13, 51, 78, 79
   H. macrophylla 42
   H. anomala petiolaris 10, 42, 49, 56

Ilex aquifolium 78
illusions 17–25
Impatiens 50, 58, 61, 63 65, **92**
insecticides 84
Ipomoea hederacea 33
Iris foetidissima 10
ivy *see Hedera*

Japanese gardens 34–5, *68, 79*
Japanese maple (*Acer*) 50
jardinières 50
Jasminum
   J. nudiflorum 10
   J. polyanthum **89**
Juncus inflexus 32
Juniperus communis 24
Kerria japonica 10
knot garden 61

Lagarosiphon major 14

Lamium 10
Lathyrus
   L. latifolius 48
   L odoratus 39
Laurus nobilis 19, 22
Lavandula angustifolia 45
lavender 49, 60, *70*, 71
Leucothoë fontanesiana 56
levels 17–18, 39, 67–8
lighting 12–13, 20, 39, 77
Ligustrum 50
   L. japonicum 19
   L. lucidum 63, **87**
Lilium 45, **93**
   L. regale 80, **93**
lily 39, 41
lily-of-the-valley (*Convallaria*) 59
Liriope
   L. muscari 35, 51, **90**
   L. muscari variegata 35
Lonicera 41
   L. x brownii 10
   L. fragrantissima 48
   L. japonica 56
   L. nitida 10, 11, 71, 72
   L. tellmanniana 10
   L. tragophylla 10
Lysimachia 57
   L. nummularia 45, 55

Mahonia 10, 42
   M. aquifolium 56, 59
   M. japonica 59, 71, 85
maintenance 82–5
   front gardens 44
   Japanese-style gardens 34
   kitchen window gardens 63
   low-maintenance gardens 69,
    72–3
   pools 14
   roof gardens 80
   side passages 53
   trompe l'oeil gardens 24
Melianthus major 71, 80
Mesembryanthemum 48
mirrors 14, *20,* 48, 62

Miscanthus sacchariflorus 15
morning glory (*Ipomoea*) 33
Muscari 35, **93**
Myriophyllum 14

Nandina domestica 63, 66
Narcissus 35, 40, 45, 61, **93**
Nictoiana sylvestris 59

oat grass (*Helictotrichon*) 32, 91
objets trouvés 9, 30–1
Ophiopogon planiscapus 45, **91**
Osmanthus 50, 56, 85

Pachysandra terminalis 61
painting
   trellis 33
   walls 9–10, 19
Palm-lily (*Cordyline*) **92**
pansies 41
Parrotia persica 60
Parthenocissus 49
   P. henryana 10
   P. quinquefolia 10
passageways 47–53
paths 19, 40
Patience plant (*Impatiens*) 50, 58,
   61, *65,* 92
paving 28, 44
paviours 69
Pelargonium 41, 48, *56, 77,* 80, *84*
perennials 90–1
perspective 19
pests 13, 84–5
Phalaris arundinacea 19
Phormium 32
   P. cookianum 72
   P. tenax 27, 43
Phyllostachys 10
Pileostegia viburnoides 10
Pinus
   P. densiflora 35
   P. mugo 35
   P. nigra 76
Pittosporum 43, 67, 71, 79, 85
   P. tobira 48, 80, **87**

planting 85
platforms 24, 31, 55
Pleioblastus
   P. variegatus **91**
   P. viridistriatus 35, **91**
Polypodium vulgare 53
Polystichum setiferum 53
ponds 14, *50, 55,* 70
pots 29–30, 51, 52
   see also adornments
primroses 61
Primula x *polyantha 35*
privacy 43, 66–7
privet 42, 57
propagation 85
pruning 85
Prunus 6, 67
   P. laurocerasus 10, 56
   P. lusitanica 10, 50
   P. subhirtella 42
Pulmonaria 10
   P. longifolia 91
   P. officinalis **90–1**
pyracantha 10, 31
Pyrus salicifolia 67

raised beds 10, 39, *47,* 48, 50, 72
Redbud tree (*Cercis*) 60
Red parrot-beak (Clianthus) **89**
Rhamnus
   alaternus 41, 72, 85
   frangula 71
rhododendron 10
Robinia pseudoacacia 67
roof gardens 75–80
Rosa 38, 41, 45, 71, 80, **88–9**
   feeding 44, 83
   R. banksia 38
   shade tolerant 60
rosemary (*Rosmarinus*) 42, 51, 71
roses *see Rosa*
Rosmarinus 42, 71, 72
   R. officinalis 51
Ruta graveolens 72

Salix 67

Salvia farinacea 71, **92**
Sarcococca 10, 50, 59–60
  S. humilis 48, 85
saxifrage 40
Scaevola aemula 58, 80, **92**
scent 49, 59–60, 70–1
Schizophragma hydrangeoides 10, **90**
Scilla siberica **93**
sculptures 19, 27, 28
  see also adornments
sea buckthorn (*Hippophae*) 76
seats 39, *70*
security 38–9
Sempervivum 32
  S. arachnoideum 25
  S. tectorum 25
shade 10, 43, 50, 60, 63
shelter 75–6
shrubs 87–9
side passages 52–3
Sisyrinchium 40
  S. striatum 45
  S. striatum variegatum 35
Skimmia 10, *45*, 50
  S. japonica 63
snowy mespilus (*Amelanchier*) 86
soil, sunken gardens 55–6
Solanum 20
  S. crispum 22, 85
  S. jasminoides 80, 85, **90**
spurge (*Euphorbia*) 90
Stachys byzantina 45, 69
stained-glass windows 23
statues 19, *23*, 32
  see also adornments
steps 11, *11*, 17–18, 24, 60–1
stones 28–9, 31, 69
sunken gardens 39, 55–63
surfaces 68, 77
sweet pea (*Lathyrus*) 19, 33, 39

Taxus 10
Tellima 10
  T. grandiflora 39
Teucrium chamaedrys 45
throughways 47–53

Thuja plicata 76
Thunbergia alata 33
Thymus x *citriodorus 45*
tobacco plant (*Nicotiana*) 59
Tolmeia menziesii 48
Trachelospermum jasminoides 72, 80, **90**
Trachycarpus fortunei **91**
trees 86–7
treillage 32
trellis 12, 32–3, 47, 52, 66, 75
trompe l'oeil 9, 18, 22–3, *23*, 24–5, 49
Tulipa **93–4**

urns 28, 79

Valeriana 51
Verbena 48, 80, **92**
Viburnum
  V. acerifolium 10
  V. davidii 10
  V. tinus 72
Vinca 10, 43
  V. minor 57
Viola 40, 55
  V. cornuta 80
Virginia creeper (*Parthenocissus*) 10, 49, 50
visual tricks 17–25
Vitis 32
  V. coignetiae 10

wall fountains *23*, 32, *65*
walls 9–10, 19, 24, 48–9, 56, 72
water 20, 32
water gardens 14–15, 70
watering 78, 83
weeping silver pear (*Pyrus*) 67
willow (*Salix*) 67
wind, roof gardens 75–6
window boxes 23, 78
windows 23, 48, 80, *80*

yew 43
yucca 32

ACKNOWLEDGMENTS

The publisher would like to thank the following photographers and organizations for their kind permission to reproduce the photographs in this book:

1 Marianne Majerus (Designer: Stephen Woodhams); 2–3 Jerry Harpur (Designer: Andrew Weaving); 4–5 Clive Nichols (Designer: Sheila Jackson); 6 Liz Eddison; 7 Marianne Majerus (Owners: Mr & Mrs Brian-Barclay)/Conran Octopus; 8 Clive Nichols (Designer: Anne Dexter); 9 John Glover/The Garden Picture Library; 10 Michelle Garrett/Insight London; 11 Marianne Majerus (Designer: Thomasina Beck); 12 Karl Dietrich-Bühler/Elizabeth Whiting & Associates; 13 Jerry Harpur (Designer: Malcolm Hillier); 16 Jerry Harpur (Designer: Jill Billington); 17 Schöner Wohnen/Camera Press; 18 Jerry Harpur (Designer: Robert Watson); 19 Noel Kavanagh (Owner: Camilla Shivarg)/Conran Octopus; 20–21 Christopher Simon-Sykes/Camera Press; 20 Above left Brigitte Thomas; 22 Andrew Lawson; 23 above Marianne Majerus/The Garden Picture Library; 23below Noel Kavanagh (Designer: Camilla Shivarg)/Conran Octopus; 26 Michele Lamontagne (Designer: Erwan Tymen); 27 Marianne Majerus (Designer: Thomasina Tarling)/Conran Octopus; 28 Noel Kavanagh (Designer: Angela Kirby)/Conran Octopus; 29 Vincent Motte (Owner: Robert Reyre); 30 left Jerry Harpur (Designer: Mel Light); 30–31 Vincent Motte (Owner: Bruno Carles); 31 right John Glover (Designer: Dan Pearson); 32 Steven Wooster/The Garden Picture Library (Designers: Duane Paul Design Team); 33 Clive Nichols (Designer: Anthony Noel); 36 Stephen Robson (Owner: Michael Hunter)/Conran Octopus; 37 Stephen Robson (Owner: Michael Hunter)/Conran Octopus; 38 above Clive Nichols (8, Malvern Terrace, London); 38 below Marianne Majerus (Designer: Thomasina Tarling)/Conran Octopus; 39 Linda Burgess/ The Garden Picture Library; 40 Neil Holmes/The Garden Picture Library; 40–41 Annette Schreiner; 42 Clive Nichols (Designer: Jean Bishop); 43 Marianne Majerus; 46 Marianne Majerus (Designer: Thomasina Tarling)/Conran Octopus; 47 Jerry Harpur (Designer: Mark Rumary); 48 Jerry Harpur (Designers: Simon Fraser and Sara Robinson); 49 Brigitte Thomas (Designer: Mr Delgado); 50 Ron Sutherland/The Garden Picture Library; 51 Jerry Harpur (Designer: John Patrick); 54 Annette Schreiner (Designer: François Bonnin); 55 Annette Schreiner (Designer: François Bonnin); 56 Annette Schreiner; 57 Steven Wooster; The Garden Picture Library (Designer: Annie Wilkes); 58 Sunniva Harte (Designer: Nigel L. Philips); 59 Marianne Majerus; 60 *Abitare*/Christine Tiberghien; 60–61 Tommy Candler; 64 Marianne Majerus (Designer: Thomasina Tarling)/Conran Octopus; 65 Marianne Majerus (Designer: Thomasina Tarling)/Conran Octopus; 66 above Jerry Harpur (Designers: Simon Fraser and Sara Robinson); 66 below Jerry Harpur (Designer: Greg Abramowitz); 67 Jerry Harpur (Designer: Lisette Pleasance); 68 Jerry Harpur (March Peter Keane); 69 Jerry Harpur (Designer: Robert Watson); 70 Jerry Harpur (Designer: Lisette Pleasance); 71 Neil Holmes (Designer: Colin Campbell); 74 Marianne Haas/Scoop; 75 Schöner Wohnen/Camera Press; 76 Jerry Harpur (Designer: Keith Corlett); 77 Simon Kenny/*Belle Magazine*; 78 Paul Ryan (Owner: Ian Hay/Conran Octopus; 79 Béatrice Pichon (Designer: Patrick Muguet); 83 Marianne Majerus (Designer: Stephen Woodhams); 84 Linda Burgess/The Garden Picture Library; 85 Stephen Hamilton